Sea
Disasters
and
Inland
Catastrophes

OTHER BOOKS BY EDWARD ROWE SNOW

Sea Disasters and Inland Catastrophes

Edward Rowe Snow

DODD, MEAD & COMPANY
NEW YORK

1   2   3   4   5   6   7   8   9   10

Library of Congress Cataloging in Publication Data

Snow, Edward Rowe.
  Sea disasters and inland catastrophes.

  Includes index.
  1. Shipwrecks. I. Title.
G525.S5796   904'.7   80-23876
ISBN 0-396-07908-3

TO
MARGARET HACKETT

whose personal aid in unearthing
elusive facts at the Boston Athenaeum
we should never forget

Contents

Part Four: 1850–1900

Part Five: 1900–1940

Part Six: 1940–Present

Preface

In almost every one of the stories or books I have written, including the smaller booklets, pamphlets and maps I have turned out since 1935, it has been my plan never to offer you a tale you can discover in one of my volumes still in print. Quite often I receive letters asking that a particularly unusual tale be inserted into an upcoming book so that those of younger generations can read it. As the years go by, these stories seem to take on new meaning for those who have read my earlier volumes and continue to read my work.

In *Sea Disasters and Inland Catastrophes* it is once again my pleasure to include tales of storms, pirates, buried treasure, ghosts, lighthouses and shipwrecks—the subjects which have attracted me the most. I trust that this year's selection will intrigue and entertain you.

I would like to thank my wife for her help and the many institutions of learning which have been great sources of inspiration: the Ventress, the Scituate, Hingham and Boston libraries, the Boston Athenaeum, the American Antiquarian Society and the Bostonian Society. Individuals who have helped me, in addition to those who plead anonymity, include Philip McNiff, Susie Withol, Bernard L. Spy, Irwin Smith, Dorothy Snow Bicknell, Eunice Snow, Victoria Snow, Donald B. Snow, Winthrop Snow, Len Bicknell, Laura Bicknell, Jessica Bicknell, Charles Wood, Melina Herron Oliver, William Pyne, Frederick G. C. Clow, Richard Carlisle, Arthur Cun-

ningham, Marie Hansen, James Douglass, Walter Spahr
Ehrenfield, Jean Foley, Trevor Johnson, Joseph Kolb, Joel
O'Brien, Larry Molignano, Richard Nikashian, Charles Marks,
Elva Ruiz, Helen Salkowski, Frederick Sanford, Chester Shea,
Alfred Schroeder, William Smits, Cheryl LaBrecque and
Caroline Phillips. John R. Herbert, Quincy banker and histo-
rian, again has given me important suggestions of vital inter-
est.

Edward Rowe Snow
Marshfield, Massachusetts

Part One

1600s

1

Bendall, America's First Scuba Diver

The name Edward Bendall often comes up in correspondence to me. Without question, scuba expert Bendall found substantial treasure in Boston Harbor in the seventeenth century, although in a strange way he also put it there. And he left far more than he removed.

More than 3¼ centuries ago a Puritan galleon holding a delightful amount of treasure blew up and sank in Boston Harbor, in the area between Charlestown and the North End. This terrible explosion aboard the *Mary Rose*, the first great marine calamity in Massachusetts history, caused underwater explorer Edward Bendall to carry out plans for constructing a diving bell. He used this device successfully to go to the bottom of Boston Harbor and remove the wreckage of the *Mary Rose*. The manner in which Bendall did this gave him the honor of being America's first diver to use a method that could be compared to the *s*elf-*c*ontained *u*nderwater *b*reathing *a*pparatus—scuba—of today.

In the summer of 1914, while exploring the stacks at the Boston Public Library under the watchful eye of Pierce Buckley, I discovered information concerning the explosion of the galleon *Mary Rose* and Bendall's diving apparatus. At the time I had been diving and experimenting with staying underwater. In my hometown of Winthrop I was possibly the only person interested enough in underwater exploration to go overboard using rubber hose and five-gallon cans. I was anxious to stay on the bottom, under the small schooners then bringing granite into the town's Crystal Bay landing at Lewis Wharf, in back of Merryman's store. I never thought of treasure in those days. But the story I gleaned at the library activated my lifelong interest in what riches might possibly be buried on the ocean floor.

In 1642 Boston Harbor had a very different appearance than it does today. The North Street area included a pier and a stone landing at the harbor end of the street. It was there that shoemaker George Burden placed a huge wooden barrel to hold water, so that he could moisten the leather he employed in his work. Farther down North Street was the slaughterhouse of Richard Nash, who often annoyed his neighbors by killing and dressing his beasts in the street. A short distance away was the home of Edward Bendall, who owned the town dock.

Bendall probably arrived in Boston on one of the four craft brought into Massachusetts by John Winthrop. (His name is spelled at least three different ways in the records.) Within two years of arriving in Boston he had so far advanced in the community that he is mentioned twice by the clerk of the colony, William Pynchon.

The first item involves the *"lighterage of ordnance."* Bendall was paid fifteen shillings for this, and received payment of two pounds, six shillings for taking *"280 bullets out of the Griffen, being 4 tides."*

Four years later the General Court Records show that it was *"Ordered that there shall be 20£ [20 pounds] gyven Edward Bendall out of the treasury towards the loss of his lighterman."*

And about six months after that: *"Whereas Edward Bendall*

had 20£ yielded toward the loss of the lighter, and the lighter
was recovered, the court allowed him 12£ of the 20£ which hee
should have had if it had not been lost towards his charge and
hindrance."

There was so much trade in Boston at this time that the
business of lighterman (now called longshoreman) was large
enough for a man to support himself by it alone. Every available foot of wharfage was needed, and so the lighters were
employed to unload cargo from ships anchored in the harbor.

Ferries to and from Boston have been given much business
down through the years, and in 1633 Bendall signed a contract
that he would "keepe a sufficient ferry boat to carry to Noodles
Island [East Boston] and to the shipps ryding before the
towne, taking for a single person iid. [twopence] and for twoe
3d. [threepence], and if there be more id. [onepence] a peece."

Edward Bendall belonged for a while to the first church, but
along with many others he later fell under the influence of
Anne Hutchinson, antagonist of John Winthrop. Church and
state strode hand in hand in those days, and because of Mrs.
Hutchinson, Bendall was deprived of his rights as a citizen. He
was also fined 40 shillings for an offense, the nature of which
has not come down to us.

In 1634 he became one of the freemen of the colony. Under
the charter the power of electing the governor was given to the
freemen, plus the privilege of deliberating on other subjects.

On March 21, 1636, Bendall was elected one of Boston's
fence viewers, a relatively important position. He and John
Button were to oversee the fences in the millfield, what is now
known as the North End.

On Christmas Day 1637, barely a year after his wife, Anne,
gave birth to a son they named Freegrace, she died. Some time
later he remarried. Bendall then built a new storehouse down
by the Town Cove and also purchased the wharf at the end of
the Cove, calling it Bendall's Dock.

Then occurred what must have been the greatest achieve-
ment of his lifetime, the raising of the sunken galleon *Mary*

Rose. Blown up by gunpowder as she was riding at anchor before the town, she is mentioned in the *Journal of Governor Winthrop,* who described the accident that took place July 27, 1640:

"Being the second day of the week, the *Mary Rose,* a ship of Bristol, of about 200 tons, her master one Captain Davis, lying before Charlton [Charlestown], was blown in pieces with her own powder, being 21 barrels; wherein the judgment of God appeared, for the master and company were many of them profane scoffers at us, at the ordinances of religion here; so as, our churches keeping a fast for our native country, etc., they kept aboard at their common service, when all the rest of the masters came to our assemblies; likewise the Lord's day following; and a friend of his going aboard next day and asking him, why he came not on shore to our meetings, his answer was, that he had a family of his own, etc., and they had as good service aboard as we had on shore.

"Within two hours after this (being about dinner time) the powder took fire (no man knows how) and blew all up, the captain and nine or ten of his men, and some four or five strangers. There was a special providence that they were aboard at that time, and some were in a boat near the ship, and others diverted by a sudden shower of rain, and others by other occasions.

"There was one man saved, being carried up in the scuttle, and so let fall in the same into the water, and being taken up by the ferry boat, near dead, he came to himself the next morning, but could not tell anything of the blowing up of the ship, or how he came there.

"The rest of the dead bodies were found, much bruised and broken. Some goods were saved, but the whole loss was estimated at 2000 pounds. A 20s. [shilling] piece was found sticking in a chip, for there was above 300 pounds in money on her, and 15 tons of lead, and 10 pieces of ordnance, which a year after were taken up and the hull of the ship was drawn ashore."

The church members of Boston considered the disaster retribution for the past sins and offenses of many seafaring men. John Endicott, who cut the cross from the English flag, wrote to John Winthrop concerning the disaster:

Dearest Sir,—Hearing of the remarkable stroak of God's hand uppon the shippe and the shippe's companie of Bristol, as also of some Atheisticall passages and hellish profanations of the Sabbaths and deriding of the people and ways of God, I thought good to desire a word or two of you of the truth of what you have heard. God will be honoured in all dealings. We have heard of several ungodly carriadges in that shippe as ffirst in their way overbound they would constantlie jeere at the holie brethren of New England, and some of the marriners would in a scoff ask when they should come to the holie Land? That the last ffast the master or captain of the shippe, with most of the companie would not goe to the meetings, but read the book of common prayer so often over that one of the companie said he had worn that thread bare, with many such passages.

Now if these or the like be true, as I am persuaded some them are, I think the truth herof would be made knowen, by some faithfull hand in Bristoll or elsewhere, ffor it is a very remarkable and unusuall stroake.

Yours ever assured.
Jo. Endicott.

Salem the 28th of the 5th month, 1640.

Thomas Lechford, the Boston lawyer, considered the case "not so much as a special providence, being by no means a friend to the Puritans and their ways." He notes in his diary the fact of the explosion, and the death of one James Smith. Later, he wrote to a friend:

"And now, Worthy Sir, what news can I write you from us, but such as is heavy and sad in every respect? Yesterday being the 27th of July, a tall ship riding at anchor before Charles-towne, that brought hither provisions from Bristoll, called the *Mary Rose,* was (most part) blown up with gun powder which she had in her for her defence, (and the rest sunke downe immediately,) through some careless rummaging with candle light in the hold: wherin died a brave mariner Captain Davis, with ten others, seamen, and two or three of the country being on boarde. Fourteen others of the ship's company being on shore, through the mercy of God escaped: I never hear such a fearful blow: it shook the house wherein I was being a mile off, as an earthquake. A sad and doleful accident, and much laid to heart by me. This was at one a clocke in the afternoone. God of his mercy grant that we the living may lay it to heart and repent indeed, lest we likewise perish."

As a result of the explosion the General Court contracted with Bendall to rid the river and harbor of the wreck.

". . . If he cleare the harbor, hee is to have all wch he can get up; if not he is to have one halfe and the country is to have the other halfe. For the clearing of the harbor he hath liberty till the first of the 8th M, 1642; and he is to give account to the treasurer, from time to time, and to leave the full haulfe, or give good security.

"Edward Bendall hath liberty to make use of any of the cables, and other things belonging to the worke, as he needeth, allowing hurt of them."

Although cables were necessary, it was not by them alone that the galleon *Mary Rose* was relieved of her cargo, ordnance and lead. Edward Bendall invented and constructed diving bells, "two great tubs, bigger than a butt, very tight, and open at one end, upon which there were hanged so many weights as would sink it to the ground (600wt)." Bendall so carefully laid his plans that he could go down and make fast the "cables and other things" to the ordnance, and put the ballast and the lead into a net or tub so that they were easily drawn up into the great lighter on the surface.

As the giant cannon came to the surface, the lightermen were very curious, for there was a rumor that substantial treasure had been hidden in some way among the guns. Many believed it to be inside the giant mouth of one of the guns, but others scoffed at the idea.

Bendall had heard the rumor. After a casual search of each

cannon, he decided it was false. From one gun he removed a large padding of rope yarn that felt unusually heavy, but it had been underwater more than two years and was soggy and foul.

Actually, the rope yarn concealed the great treasure. But Bendall, who could not quite understand how the galleon's commanders would ever put valuable gold and silver coins inside a cannon's mouth, ordered that the rope yarn be "flung aside."

Then came the day Bendall decided to test the cannon. He rammed the rope yarn inside the gun as a firing wad. At high tide the cannon was fired. Myriads of coins shot out from the wad as it described a parabola, raining down into the water in both deep and shallow areas.

The next day at low tide those walking along the sandy beach in the vicinity of the firing were amazed to see gold and silver coins glistening in the sand. During the next few days hikers picked up no less than fifteen pounds of the gold and silver. When Bendall learned of this, he rightfully claimed the money as his. The finders would not give up the treasure. "Whereupon," says Winthrop, Bendall brought "his action and the money was adjudged to him." *

Evidently Winthrop was quite impressed with Bendall's ability. In Volume II of *Winthrop's Journal* he explains the inner workings of the bell. Bendall would go down in the diving bell and would sit inside, "a cord in his hand to give notice when they should draw him up, and another cord to show when they should remove it from place to place, so he could continue in his tub near half an hour, and fasten ropes to the ordnance, and put the lead, etc., into a net or tub. And when the tub was drawn up, one knocked on the head of it, and thrust a long pole under water, which the diver laid hold of, and so was drawn up by it; for they might not draw the open end out of water for endangering him, etc."

* In today's values, possibly $100,000 is still on the bottom of Boston Harbor, where it landed after the gun fired centuries ago.

Having done so well with the diving bell, Bendall asked the General Court for a patent. He was refused, although no one in America had ever constructed such a device before.

All the material Bendall brought up was stored at Castle Island. On September 7, 1643, "it was ordered by the court that Edward Bendall should fetch away the ordnance, ammunition, lead and other utensals from the Castle Island and deliver what is granted to Charlestown, and rest to Boston."

The name of Edward Bendall is not found in the records after 1660. He died about then, but it is not known where or precisely when. Bendall's son, Freegrace, and his wife Mary were lost at sea, leaving five children "soe small not able to shift for them selves" to be cared for by the town.

2

Mount Agamenticus

Lofty Mount Agamenticus, not far from York, Maine, is the highest mountain in the region. It is the outstanding landmark for sailors sixty miles up and down the coast, rearing its giant back almost at the edge of the sea, into which it seems to be advancing. Its form is at once graceful and imposing.

As Samuel Adams Drake related in 1891, Mount Agamenticus is the extreme outpost of the great White Mountains. No mariner could ever mistake Agamenticus for any other location, for it stands as the solitary guidepost of a natural harbor, actually the only real harbor for some distance around.

Poet James Russell Lowell in his "Pictures from Appledore" makes this reference to Agamenticus, the sailor's mountain:

> He glowers there to the north of us
> Wrapt in his mantle of blue haze,
> Unconvertibly savage, and scorns to take
> The white man's baptism on his ways.
> Him first on shore the coaster divines
> Through the early gray, and sees him shake
> The morning mist from his scalp-lock of pines:
> Him first the skipper makes out in the west,
> Ere the earliest sunstreak shoots tremulous,

Flashing with orange the palpitant lines
Of mutable billow, crest after crest,
And murmurs *Agamenticus!*
As if it were the name of a saint.

The name is in fact a legacy of the Indians who dwelt at its foot, and who always invested the mountain with a sacred character. From this circumstance comes the Indian legend of Saint Aspenquid, whom some writers have identified with the patriarch Passaconaway, the hero of so many wonderful exploits in healing and in necromancy.

The Indian name of the pond at the source of the York River is Añghemak-ti-koos, or Snowshoe, as the pond is in the shape of a snowshoe. For countless centuries before the white man came, the entire area around the mountain was called Agamenticus, but now the name is confined to the mountain itself.

Early in the seventeenth century, as far as can be proved, Sir Ferdinando Gorges established a colony at the mouth of the Agamenticus River, now known as York. He bought twenty-four thousand acres of land, half on each side of the small tidal river, and gave his grandson management of the colony.

Edward Godfrey, who settled on the Agamenticus River in 1632, petitioned the General Court in Massachusetts in 1654 that he had been a "well wisher, encourager, and furderer of this colony of New England, for forty-five years past, and above thirty-two years an adventurer on that design, twenty-four years an inhabitant of this place, the first that ever bylt or settled ther." Two years later he obtained from the Plymouth council a grant of twelve thousand acres of land on the north side of the River Agamenticus.

The York area was made into a city by Sir Ferdinando Gorges on March 1, 1641; the first election of mayor and aldermen was held March 25, 1642. The city of three hundred residents was called Georgeana, and Thomas Gorges was elected mayor. *

Thus, according to Edward C. Moody, Agamenticus became "the first incorporated English city on the American continent, with the graceful name of Georgeana." Unfortunately, in 1652 the Massachusetts Puritans found that two factions were attempting to run Georgeana, and intervened to annex the Agamenticus area to Massachusetts.

Gorges's complicated machinery was thus overthrown in a short time. The province became a county with the name of Yorkshire, while the metropolis of Georgeana from that moment on was called York.

York had many problems in the seventeenth century. One embarrassing situation was finally solved when an erring, amorous preacher, the Reverend Mr. George Burdett, was shipped back to London. An idea of what Burdett stood for can be gained by the remarks of Samuel Adams Drake:

"On looking about him Deputy Gorges found neither law, order, nor morality prevailing,—a state of things not to be wondered at when it is known that the minister himself, George Burdett, not only set his parishioners an example of unchaste conduct, but easily distanced them in the number and shamelessness of his amours."

Scarcely had the memories of Burdett faded when the terrible King Philip's War was upon New England. This was followed fifteen years later—on February 5, 1692—by the Abenaki uprising.

A violent snowstorm was falling that day. At the height of the storm three hundred Abenaki Indians attacked the village, bursting into the homes one by one. Ransacking the houses, they ripped up the beds and set fire to them, so that shortly twenty houses were ablaze. When the slaughter ended, only

* The aldermen were Edward Godfrey, Roger Garde, George Puddington, Bartholomew Bartness, Edward Johnson, Arthur Bragdon, Henry Simpson and John Rogers.

eighty people were still alive, many of whom were carried off into captivity. The Abenaki killed about seventy-five residents and left only four buildings standing: the garrison houses of Alcock, Harmon, Norton and Preble. Cotton Mather called the Indians "bloody Tygres," and he also mentions the shooting of the Reverend Mr. Shubael Dummer, who lived on the seaside near Roaring Rock. While his wife and son were carried off into captivity, "one of the hell hounds" strutted amidst the prisoners wearing the minister's clothing.

A boy of four survived the massacre. Many years later he led an avenging band against the same Abenaki Indians, exterminating both the Kennebec tribe and their mission. His name was Jeremiah Moulton.

More than a century before the Abenaki uprising, the gallant Saint Aspenquid, an Indian, was born in the region of Mount Agamenticus in 1588. He was about ninety when he died. Converted to Christianity and baptized when he was about forty years old, he dedicated his life to active ministration among the people of his own race, to whom he became a saint and a prophet. For more than forty years he is said to have wandered east to west, north to south, preaching the gospel to no less than sixty-six different Indian nations. Saint Aspenquid healed the sick and performed many miracles that gave him the character of a prophet appointed by Heaven. Even the white man agreed that he was endowed with supernatural powers.

Finally came the period of extreme old age. The venerable patriarch knew that he must soon be gathered to his fathers. Saint Aspenquid at last came home to spend his final days among his own people. When he died, all the sachems of the different tribes came together to attend the funeral of this greatest of all Maine Indians. They carried the body of their prophet to the summit of Mount Agamenticus.

Before burying the patriarch there, following the sacred customs of the period, the hunters of each tribe spread through-

out the forests to catch wild beasts—among them deer, rabbit,
bear, buffalo, moose, porcupine, woodchuck, weasel, otter and
mountain lion—and to slaughter them as a sacrifice in honor
of the departed saint. Even the fishermen of the region made
their contributions.

Poet John Albee wrote:

SAINT ASPENQUID

The Indian hero, sorcerer, and saint,
   Known in the land as Passaconaway,
And after called the good Saint Aspenquid,
   Returning, travel worn and spent with age
From vain attempt to reconcile his race
   With ours, sent messengers throughout the East
To summon all the blood-bound tribes to him;
   For that upon the ancient meeting-place,
The sacred mountain Agamenticus,
   When next the moon should show a new-bent bow,
He there would celebrate his funeral feast
   With sacrifices due and farewell talk. . . .

Light not the fires of vengeance in your hearts,
   For sure the flame will turn against yourselves,
And you will perish utterly from earth.
   Nor yet submit too meekly, but maintain
The valorous name once ours in happy days.
   Be prudent, wise, and slow to strike.
Fall back; seek other shores and hunting grounds,—
   I cannot bear you perish utterly!
Though, looking through the melancholy years,
   I see the end, but turn my face away,
So heavy are my eyes with unshed tears;
   And yours too I would turn, warriors and braves!
And mind not my prophetic vision much,—
   Th'unhappy gift of him who lives too long;
But mind the counsel many years have taught,
   The last I give: remember it, and live!

3

The Gorges
of Maine

When I authored *Fantastic Folklore and Fact* several years ago, I dedicated it to Dr. Robert E. Moody. On December 27, 1977, he wrote to tell me that the Maine Historical Society was about to publish his book *The Letters of Thomas Gorges, 1640–1642.**

Dr. Moody sent along a copy of one of the letters that tells about a shipwreck of which I had never heard. Although colonial Governor John Winthrop mentions the wreck, Dr. Moody said it was his pleasure to give me all the details for the first time. "I take great pride in being able to tell Edward Snow things he doesn't know about wrecks."

The narrative of the disaster is included in a letter written by Thomas Gorges to Sir Ferdinando Gorges, his cousin, dated May 19, 1642 (original spelling retained):

"We have had a most intollerable peircing winter that the like was never known by Inglish or Indian. It is incredible to relate the extremity of the weather. Fouls & fish lay frozen

---

*The letters were written from York, Maine, where on my 1978 Flying Santa trip I landed for the first time in a helicopter, to say hello to the people of Cape Neddick Nubble.

Flotinge thicke on the waters in the sea. For 10 weeks not a
boat caught a fish, the Isles of Shoals excepted, where they
have had the best fishinge that ever was there known, some
10, some 11,000 of fish & upward to a boat, the largest that
ever was seen.

"I will relate you one sad story of the extremity of the
weather by which you may beleeve the rest. On the 23 of
January, Alderman Longe his eldest son, with our provost
martiall named Robert Sankey, Will Cutts, brother to the litle
boy, one brown, Gibbins, Lacy & Heard went to sea & soe wer
driven in a storme till the 27, cast all theyr victualls over board
except one side of porke & a little meal in which tyme . . .
neither ate a bit nor drank a drop expecting every hour to
sinke, The water soe Frose in theyr boat, but by Gods goodenss
they got a shore on Monhigun an Iland to the eastward, wher
they lay frozen in most miserable case, not one able to help
another, having lost all theyr victualls, one side of porke & a
little meal. 5 days after, Cutts died next Lacy, then Sankey,
last Heard. The rest wer brought hither by a boat that [was]
goinge a fishinge . . . [whose?] own boat was spared . . . spied
them after 5 weeks time. Mr Longe & Gibbons are thoroughly
recovered, Brown hath lost 3 Joynts. To relate all that passed of
theyr misery would seem rather some things fained than
reall."

On many occasions I have written about Sir Ferdinando, to
whom the preceding letter was addressed. A most interesting
figure in the Maine-stream of history, he was leader of the
Plymouth Company and proprietor of Maine. He was also one
of the two chief backers of the Sagadahoc colony.

The expedition to found that colony was fitted out by Sir
Ferdinando. The *Gift of God,* captained by George Popham,
and the *Mary and John,* under the control of Raleigh Gilbert,
sailed May 1, 1607, and June 1, respectively. They dropped
anchor north of Monhegan Island August 7, then sailed to
Popham Beach on the Sagadahoc River, which is the lower

Kennebec, on August 14. Here they built a fort and established the colony. Because of idleness and factionalism, the settlement failed on the death of George Popham the next year.

Sir Ferdinando died in 1647. On March 13, 1677, John Usher, agent of Massachusetts, bought out the rights to Maine from the Gorges heirs for 1250 pounds. Maine stayed incorporated with Massachusetts until March 15, 1820.

Richard B. Morris, in his *Encyclopedia of American History* (page 36), includes this letter written in 1642: "Despite the attempt of Gorges to govern Maine through his cousin Thomas Gorges and the establishment of a provincial court at York, (25 June 1640), Massachusetts persisted in its expansionist aims."

4

Treasure in Byfield,
Massachusetts

I have spent scores of years, gone hundreds of miles and suffered crushing disappointments to produce this chapter. The stories of John Winthrop, Mary Sholy, William Schooler, Orin Arlin, Dr. Griffin and Stearns Compton span different generations and even different centuries. The unifying thread is the rock marked *A*, which probably still exists in Byfield, Massachusetts. But whether or not any of us shall ever see it is another question. Despite my intense efforts to garner more details from several generations of writers and oral storytellers, the key moments lack the completeness they deserve.

John Winthrop, writing in his 1637 Journal, tells us that William Schooler was a common adulterer who "had wounded a man in a duel" and had been forced to flee "into this country, leaving his wife (a handsome, neat woman) in England." Winthrop goes on:

> He lived with another fellow in Merrimack, and there being a poor maid at Newbury, one Mary Sholy, who had desired a guide to go with her to her master, who dwelt at Pascataquack, he inquired her out, and agreed for fifteen shillings to conduct her thither. But two days after, he returned, and, being asked why he returned so

soon, he answered that he had carried her within two or three miles of the place, and then she would go no farther. Being examined for this by the magistrate at Ipswich, and no proof found against him, he was let go. But, about a year after, being impressed to go against the Pequods, he gave ill speeches, for which the governor sent warrant for him, and being apprehended (and supposed it had been for the death of the maid, some spake what they had heard, which might occasion suspicion,) he was again examined, and divers witnesses produced about it. Whereupon he was committed, arraigned, and condemned, by due proceedings.

John Winthrop relates that not only had Schooler lived a vicious life, but he was then living as an atheist. He had sought out the maid, and taken her to a place where he had never been, and had crossed the Merrimack three miles from the usual path. But he claimed that he had gone close to Swamscote, where he left her. When he returned he had blood on his hat and clothes, which he claimed "was with a pigeon" that he killed. He had a scratch on the left side of his nose and claimed it was from a "bramble, which could not be," as the scratch was too wide, and he then said "it was with his piece [gun]."

About half a year later the body of the maid was found by an Indian in the depths of a thick swamp, "ten miles short of the place he said he left her in," and about three miles from the place where he crossed the "Merrimack, (and it [the body] was after seen, by the English,) the flesh being rotted off it, and the clothese laid in a heap by the body."

Schooler afterward claimed that he met with a bear and thought the bear might kill her, yet would not go back to save her.

Put in prison, Schooler escaped but later was apprehended near Powder Horn Hill. Winthrop writes, with little detail (he completely left out the hanging incident), the conclusion of Schooler's unhappy life:

[Schooler] hid himself out of the way, for fear of pursuit, and after, when he arose to go forward, he could not, but (as he himself confessed) was forced to return back to prison again.

At his death he confessed he had made many lies to excuse himself, but denied that he had killed or ravished her. He was very loath to die, and had hope he should be reprieved; but the court held him worthy of death, in undertaking the charge of a shiftless maid, and leaving her (when he might have done otherwise) in such a place as he knew she must perish, if not preserved by means unknown. Yet there were some ministers and others who thought the evidence not sufficient to take away his life.

Winthrop indeed makes quite a case against Schooler, stressing in his Journal eleven points against him, a few being the peculiar summing up of the money the two had: "He had about ten shillings in his purse, and yet he said she would give him but seven shillings, and he carried no money with him" (Winthrop's Journal, Volume 1, pages 236–238). Another point against Schooler was his incorrect description of the road he was supposed to have taken. A third was the peculiar fact that Schooler did not mention to "anybody of her, till he was demanded of her." And so it was that he was "committed, arraigned, and condemned, by due proceeding."

Mary Sholy, who was murdered, had a strong group of followers north of Boston who firmly believed that the money mentioned by John Winthrop and connected with her death was buried along the Parker River at some unknown time between the landing of the Puritans and the publication of the *Massachusetts Spy* for March 5, May 7 and August 20, 1800. (These newspapers are available in several New England libraries.)

In the Parker River area in Byfield, Massachusetts, there is a rock marked *A*, near which many people believe a substantial treasure has been buried. The tidal river only covers the trap-granite boulder at the highest of tides, probably two or three times a year. The distinctive mark is the letter *A*, approximately six inches in height. At least a dozen stories involving the rock have been told to me orally by North Shore residents of former generations.

Miss Grace Bixby, Newburyport historian, believed that the rock was a marker to indicate the location of a hoard buried nearby, but she had no idea who had concealed the treasure or where it was. Mary Sholy may have had considerable wealth, but probably never the large number of coins so many residents who knew about the rock thought of as a possibility.

Fred Dudley Pearson wondered if the two pirate chests brought to Newburyport after the Gonaïves incident could have any connection with the rock marked A.

The tale of the pirate chests off the island of Gonaïve begins in the West Indies. Captain Roger Hayman, renegade Englishman, was in command of a pirate stronghold with headquarters at the western end of the island of Haiti. Bold and aggressive, he never worried about attacking American men-of-war when they were becalmed in the Gulf of Gonaïve. Pirates easily overcame merchantmen caught in the vicinity.

Late in December 1799, in order to halt Hayman's piracy, the United States sent a small fleet into the area. The armed schooner *Experiment,* commanded by Lieutenant William Maley, was ordered to convey four merchantmen by the island of Haiti.

On January 1, 1800, a dead calm set in. Hayman decided to attack. Ten pirate barges, each manned by forty to fifty desperadoes, set out from Haiti with Captain Hayman in command. Hayman first boarded an American merchantman and took her strongbox, then went aboard an English vessel of the convoy and took the purser's chest of sovereigns.

Before anything else could happen, the *Experiment* sailed into the area, sank three pirate craft and killed almost eighty pirates. Hayman was badly wounded; aboard the *Experiment,* one American was wounded and two injured. The frigate *Boston* came along and also attacked the pirates, crippling five more pirate vessels.

Later many Massachusetts newspapers, especially the Newburyport paper on March 5, May 7, and August 20, 1800,

gave details of the pirate battle off Gonaïve. But few Newburyport citizens realized it would have lasting repercussions
in nearby Byfield, Massachusetts.

Captain Hayman kept the two chests acquired in the recent
fighting and divided the remainder of the booty among his
followers. Soon he gained possession of another trim schooner
of 295 tons to take him to England. His wounds were very
severe, and he reached Liverpool more dead than alive.

Greatly disappointed to find that his family had emigrated to
New York, Hayman decided to start for America. He sold his
schooner and took passage on a brig that would make its first
stop in Newburyport. With great secrecy he made arrangements for the two chests to be brought on board and hidden in
the captain's cabin. A passenger on the brig, Dr. Griffin,
treated his wounds and learned of the chests of treasure.
Realizing that Hayman had only a few more days to live, the
doctor let Stearns Compton, another passenger, in on the secret. The two made plans to get the chests when they reached
port.

Compton hired a sturdy team as soon as they arrived in
Newburyport, surreptitiously transferred the treasure to the
wagon, and gave a signal to the doctor that all was ready.
Griffin jumped into the wagon and seized the reins. Compton
was soon beside him.

"I know the way," Griffin exclaimed. "We'll keep on this
road."

Two hours later they reached a small inn known as the
Pearson Tavern, situated by the side of the highway in the
parish of Byfield. The inn was run by Jeremiah Pearson, the
great-great-grandfather of Fred Dudley Pearson, whom I mentioned earlier. Pearson agreed to give Griffin and Compton
lodging for the night. The two men took turns watching the
barn where the treasure was concealed to make sure it was
safe.

Morning finally came, but with it arrived a man on horseback who rode up and told the news. "Have you heard the latest? Two men got away from a brig in Newburyport Harbor with all the purser's money and are on the way to Boston." The horseman then galloped away in the morning light.

"Gentlemen," Pearson asked, "whence came you last night?"

"From Haverhill," Griffin replied promptly. Then the two men paid their bill and drove away, taking the Andover Road until they reached the Parker River. There they stopped, determined to bury the money.

This was the very morning that a bird lover, Howard Noyes by name, had climbed a tree in the vicinity. Observing some birds in a nest, he happened to glance across and see the men when they got out of the wagon near a large boulder of trap-granite. It was hard work they planned. Compton dug with a small spade until he had a pit four feet deep, whereupon they piled the money into the hole and smoothed dirt and foliage over the top again. Then they marked the boulder with a six-inch-high A and departed the area.

High in the tree, young Noyes became frightened. He climbed down and ran home to tell his story. A search at first failed to discover anything. Later the letter A was identified on the boulder by another group.

Meanwhile the two schemers reached Boston, took the New York stage and, after parting, agreed to return and claim the treasure in five years. Half a decade brings many changes. Neither man ever returned to Byfield, and both were dead by 1857. Sixty-six years later, a great-granddaughter of Compton inherited a strange pact the two men had signed in Byfield. Compton had sealed it in an envelope with information about where he had buried the treasure. Each generation had unsealed the envelope, read the instructions and done nothing but reseal the envelope. They wanted "no part of the disgraceful matter," according to one source.

Nevertheless, this particular lady, Compton's great-granddaughter, became fascinated by the document and wrote to the Pearson Tavern, thinking she would be revealing unknown valuable information.

Of course, half of the Byfield residents interested in treasure had heard the Noyes story before. Excitement developed again and more holes were dug. But no one has proof that a treasure was found at that time.

Within the last ten years the highway in the area of the Parker River has been changed so that the rock marked *A* seems to have vanished. Long before this, actually more than half a century ago, Orin Arlin's story begins when a workman was digging a well not too far from the rock marked *A*. Arlin visited the scene and spoke to the workman.

"How are you coming with the well?"

"No water yet," came the short reply.

Late the following afternoon Orin returned. The workman had vanished, and there were indications that he had discovered something very unusual. Old oak splinters and fragments of canvas lay strewn at the bottom of the well hole, and everything pointed to a hasty exit by the laborer.

Arlin never saw the well-digger again, but one day when he was over at a store on Ring's Island, Salisbury, the proprietor spoke up. "Say, Orin, your friend the well-digger was in the other day, and look what he used for money to pay for his purchases!" The merchant held up a handful of coins, still fairly bright and shiny except for a few badly tarnished places. Orin Arlin told me about it later in detail.

"Although my friend the well-digger told the store proprietor that he got the money by winning a lottery, I really believe he blundered in some way onto the money, or at least a part of it."

Arlin later gave me one of the coins, and it now has a valued place in my collection of pirate skulls, derringers and treasure. Regardless of which story it is connected with, I know the possible bloody past of the metal disk. But Orin Arlin cautioned me against placing too much significance on the coin; he rightly suggests it may have come from anywhere.

Now, after generations and generations have passed, we at least know that some treasure has appeared. The remainder, if there is a remainder, probably is buried under the highway, not too great a distance from another buried item, a trap-granite rock marked *A*, which formerly was pointed out to visitors as they wandered along the banks of the beautiful Parker River in Byfield, Massachusetts.

Part Two

1700s

1

Shipwreck
and Cannibalism

Many of the true stories I have related through the past fifty years include details or incidents that baffle understanding. This tale is in that category, for it contains the horrible act of cannibalism. It is my belief that such an inhuman deed cannot be satisfactorily explained. All a writer can do is relate the facts, leaving the reader to his own thoughts and questions regarding the meanderings of human behavior.

In February 1765 the vessel *Amiable Suzette* sailed from Bordeaux, France, to San Domingo in the West Indies. There passenger Peter Viaud was taken desperately ill.

Peter Viaud did not improve and was put ashore at Saint Louis Island, near Cuba. After several weeks at the home of a friend, Monsieur Desclou, he recovered completely. During his illness the two men planned a journey to Louisiana to trade various goods for a considerable profit, if all worked well.

They acquired the ship *Tiger,* of which Captain La Couture was master. The *Tiger* was loaded with commodities they believed would have a good sale at their destination. Several passengers were signed up for the trip, and the captain brought his wife and son David along. The ship's company amounted to sixteen in all when they were ready for sailing.

On January 2, 1766, the *Tiger* left Saint Louis Island but was soon becalmed. Day after day there was no wind. By January 26 they were no closer to Louisiana than the Isle of Pines, some fifty miles south of the western curve of Cuba. However, the master of the *Tiger* erroneously claimed that they had reached not Cape Pepe on the Isle of Pines, but the Cape of Saint Antonio at Cuba. This serious miscalculation led to the ship crashing against rocks forming an outlying ledge northwest of the Isle of Pines.

The crew shifted the cargo several times and finally managed to free the *Tiger* from the rocks. But she had developed a bad leak, and all hands were called out to the pumps. During this crisis it was agreed that Peter Viaud should take command.

Finally the leaking ship reached Cape Antonio and started across the Gulf of Mexico, heading for the Mississippi River. The water in the hold gained to such an extent that the vessel barely kept afloat. In her helpless, waterlogged condition, the *Tiger* was caught by the approach of a violent storm. Before the storm hit, a Spanish frigate came in sight and offered assistance. Darkness intervened, however, and when morning came the frigate was gone.

The next morning the crew of the *Tiger* discovered a new leak. Bailing and pumping continued, but all aboard realized that they should attempt to run the *Tiger* ashore somewhere along the coast of Apalachee Bay in northwest Florida.

On the night of February 16 the *Tiger* again struck heavily, this time on some jagged ledges six miles from land. The waves soon tore the stern apart. When the tide rose and the *Tiger* gradually lifted herself over the ledges, it was discovered that the rudder had been ripped off.

Desperately Viaud guided the *Tiger* by the foresail. Two hours later they approached the southern shores of an unknown island, possibly Cape Saint George's. Viaud and the captain planned to cut away the masts and build a raft on which to float ashore.

Suddenly, without warning, the *Tiger* went over on her beam ends, throwing several of the crew into the sea. Most were able to swim back to the wreck, just as the rays of the moon that had been guiding them disappeared, leaving the survivors on the upturned bottom of the *Tiger* in pitch darkness.

Rain began falling and a violent thunderstorm broke loose. Higher and higher came the waves, until they washed entirely over the shipwrecked men and women. Lightning flashes illuminated the terrible scene.

Finally dawn arrived. By its faint light Viaud surveyed their situation. The waves were running very high. Shore was but a short distance away. However, Viaud knew that an attempted landing in the seething billows would end in death for most of them, for the giant breakers were rolling up on shore with terrific impact.

No one dared move for several hours, while the wreck drifted closer to shore. Finally a Dutch sailor could stand it no longer. Sliding off the ship's bottom into the heavy seas, he struck out hopefully for shore. A wave swallowed him up momentarily. He was seen again, still swimming toward land. The next wave smashed into him, and five minutes later a great comber tossed his lifeless body with dreadful violence on a rocky ledge.

Finally the storm appeared to be dying down. The masts and cordage had all washed away, so the last hopes of making a raft and floating ashore were gone. There was a tiny boat still attached to the *Tiger,* and three sailors were able to cut it free, bail it out and start for shore. They landed safely on the beach and pulled the tiny craft above the reach of the tide as dusk fell.

A short time later the *Tiger* drifted in toward shore and lodged precariously against hidden rocks, in danger of breaking up at any time. Those still clinging to the wreck could see the sailors on the beach attempting to patch up the skiff. An old sailor, watching their efforts, asked for all available pieces of cloth. Securing the pieces to himself, he plunged into the sea and managed to swim to shore. Working feverishly, the four men stuffed strips of cloth into the many cracks of the rescue craft. It was three o'clock before the boat could be launched.

Out on the capsized *Tiger,* lots were drawn to decide who would go on the first trip ashore. The four winners soon scrambled into the boat and reached land safely. Again the tiny skiff was sent out. Meanwhile, Viaud, his friend Desclou and Desclou's servant succeeded in pulling free a large fragment of the *Tiger*'s stern. They clambered aboard; ten minutes later they floated up on the beach. A short time later the skiff brought the final four survivors to shore.

After a short period of prayer and rejoicing, Viaud decided to search for food. The tide was low, and on nearby rocks he found more than enough oysters to satisfy their hunger. One man, Mate Dutroche, was too sick to benefit from the nourishment. Becoming delirious, he was in agony by morning and died before noon. The crew buried him in the sand.

Cargo from the *Tiger* soon scattered up and down the beach, including several trunks; some casks of tafia, a type of fiery liquor made of distilled sugarcane juice; and many bales of merchandise.

The ocean had calmed down. Viaud decided to return to the wreck and see what of value was still aboard. When he asked for volunteers to row out with him, not a single man came forward. Therefore, he rowed to the *Tiger* alone. He found that the craft had partly righted herself, with one section entirely above water. Viaud was able to obtain a keg of gunpowder, six muskets, a flint, a package of Indian handkerchiefs, several blankets, forty pounds of biscuits and two hatchets. Rowing ashore safely, he was received with great admiration by the others when he landed with the welcome supplies.

Ordering the crew to collect dry wood, he struck the flint and soon produced sparks to start a warm fire, around which everyone huddled. Several men had explored the island and found a spring of water, bringing back enough of the precious liquid for all. The biscuits, which had been immersed in salt water, were soaked in the fresh water for several hours, dried out by the fire, then dipped into the tafia and pronounced entirely acceptable.

The next night the survivors gathered around the fire and discussed plans for the immediate future. They were fairly certain that they had landed at Cape Saint George's Island, one of a series of islands forming an outer barrier in a southwesterly direction from what is now Franklin County, Florida.

At the time Indian tribes and wild animals controlled Florida's forest regions. Bear, deer, fox and wolves prowled the woods. It was known that the Indians of the Apalachicola area left the mainland every winter to hunt on the islands offshore until the following April, and the shipwrecked survivors feared they would be killed by the savages. This fear was heightened because of the casks of strongly alcoholic tafia, which often left Indians with such a feeling of exuberance that a massacre followed. Thus the crew staved in the barrels of liquor one by one, until they had destroyed all but three casks. Viaud ordered these buried deep in the sand for an emergency.

On February 22 a seaman who had been a few hundred yards from the camp came rushing out of the forest crying, "The Indians! The Indians! We are lost!"

Soon two Indian men and three women appeared, walking slowly toward the survivors. The men each carried a tomahawk and a musket.

Realizing that the Indians planned no immediate harm, Viaud decided to keep on friendly terms with them. He presented the women with trinkets and the men with other little gifts. Viaud ordered a cask of tafia removed from the sand, and soon the Indians and the survivors were drinking around the fire.

One of the Indians spoke a few words of Spanish. Viaud eventually learned that he was Chief Antonio, hailing from Saint Mark in the Apalachee Bay some thirty-six miles away.

Those with him were members of his immediate family. They had been wintering on a neighboring island and had found fragments of wreckage washed up on shore. Suspecting that a ship had struck the rocks in the area, they paddled over to the island to investigate.

After several pleasant hours the Indians withdrew, taking three sailors with them and promising to return the following day. The three survivors were landed on the chief's island, and he appeared the next day with food—a bustard and a roebuck—for the shipwrecked party to eat. Later that day he agreed to carry back six more survivors, including Viaud, Captain La Couture and his wife and son David. The five sailors left near the wreck were brought to Antonio's island a few days later, after the chief had gone hunting.

The chief disappeared into the island forest for the next five days. Upon his return, Viaud offered muskets and other supplies if he would take them by canoe to the mainland. Antonio countered with the proposal that he would make only one trip. He asked Viaud to pick the passengers.

Viaud chose the three members of the Couture family, Desclou, a slave and himself. Antonio took only his wife, leaving the other members of his family with the remaining sailors as good faith that he would return. Some boiled quarters of a bear and a roebuck, together with several pounds of biscuits and a container of water, were taken aboard the craft.

The following morning the canoe passengers landed at another island. Antonio decided that more provisions were needed. After days of hunting, enough oysters and wild fowl were obtained to continue the journey toward Fort Saint Marks. That night Chief Antonio brought the canoe ashore on a sandbar, bare of all trees and other vegetation. Viaud became suspicious that Antonio was planning to abandon them there. When he expressed these fears to the others, La Couture laughed and told him to forget his worries and go to sleep.

"All will be well in the morning," La Couture promised.

Shortly after midnight Viaud woke up, feeling extremely

uneasy. He rose and looked around. The fire they had built was still smoldering, but his worst fears were realized when he looked for the native's canoe. It was gone! The muskets had also been taken, leaving the shipwrecked party with only one sheath knife, a rather blunt instrument Viaud always wore at his hip. All they had were the clothes on their backs, the blankets in which they slept and one knife. Search as they could, they found nothing to satisfy their hunger.

Viaud realized that to stay on the tiny island would be to resign themselves to death. Less than half a mile to the west lay another island, and at low tide the desperate party waded and swam across to it.

Immediately they began to search for oysters. Finding plenty, they satisfied their appetites. They also discovered a tiny stream of water not far away. The hot sun came out from behind the clouds, enabling them to dry their clothes. Relatively comfortable, the party fell asleep.

When night came it was so cold that they were unable to keep warm. They got up and walked around. They grew hungry again, but the tide had come in and they were forced to wait for low water to get oysters. The only herb or roots they discovered were some wild sorrel plants. The wind changed to the southeast, and they found to their disappointment that the oyster beds did not become bare when the wind came in from that quarter. Consequently they had to wait until the following day, when the wind died down, to get oysters. After this experience they decided to keep an extra supply in reserve.

In this manner the weeks went by. On March 22 Viaud recalled having seen an old canoe on one of the islands where Antonio had stopped while hunting. This seemed the best solution to the problem of getting to Fort Saint Marks. Viaud and Captain La Couture agreed that they and Desclou should try to find the canoe.

At low tide they were able to wade back to the barren sandbar, then set out from the other side heading in a westerly direction. They had to swim in deep water to reach the island where they had seen the wreck of the canoe. It was strenuous effort for the exhausted men, but they all arrived safely and threw themselves down to rest.

The hot sun soon brought them back to life. Within the hour they were lucky enough to find the old canoe, but it was in terrible condition. They debated whether it was really worth salvaging. Seeing it as their only hope, they fell to work repairing it with osiers, or willow twigs, reinforced with Spanish beard, a tough moss that flourished in the area.

Hunger finally caused them to cease their efforts on the canoe and to turn their attention to food, which they found in a nearby oyster bed.

"I like oysters better fried or stewed," said Viaud. "There must be some way of getting a fire."

"I've got it!" cried Desclou. "Didn't we see Antonio change his flint somewhere around here?"

"Why, I think you're right!" agreed Peter. "Let's try to find the old flint."

After eating several more raw oysters, the men walked across the island to the location of their last camp with the chief. Finding the ruins of the old fire, they searched diligently until finally Viaud discovered the vital flint.

Soon they had a hot fire burning and oysters cooking. The men then lay down and slept in happy exhaustion.

Next morning they were awakened by the rising sun and again fell to work on the canoe. It was agreed that a blanket should be sacrificed and cut into strips to caulk the cracks. All that day they worked, trying to make the canoe watertight. The following morning they placed it in the water, and La Couture agreed to ferry it across to the island where the others had been left. Gingerly he stepped aboard and began to paddle; the craft still leaked considerably.

As soon as La Couture was out of sight, Viaud and Desclou explored the other side of the island seeking another way of getting to the mainland. They were unable to advance beyond the edge of a channel at least three miles wide.

Deciding to wade back to the island where Madame La Couture had set up camp, they made rapid progress and soon reached their companions. Next morning Viaud discovered a dead roebuck on the beach. Evidently it had bled to death a short time before, and Peter was able to cut it up and cook it on a spit. All ate heartily, after which they slept in comfort until the sun rose. It was March 26, 1766.

The canoe had leaked terribly, and La Couture had barely reached the island without sinking. Still anxious to repair the canoe so that they could paddle to the mainland, Viaud decided that two more blankets should be cut up to reinforce the cracks. Three days were devoted to this project.

Finally they placed the craft in the water and Viaud tested it. Feeling the planking sink under him, and watching the water begin to seep in, he decided it was hopeless. "I shall never go to sea in this craft," he declared.

"Come on, Peter," La Couture cried. "You and I can paddle while Desclou bails. We'll reach the mainland in no time."

Viaud refused to go with La Couture and Desclou. "You'll never make it in a thousand years!" he cried, and refused to help the others as they loaded a scanty stock of provisions aboard.

La Couture bade farewell to his wife and son, then instructed his slave to remain faithfully at Madame's side. He went back to the canoe, ordered Desclou to take the bow seat, got in at the stern and pushed off.

They figured that the mainland was five to six miles away. Although the two men paddled with determination, their progress was slow, for the water pouring into the tiny craft made it heavy and unwieldy. Soon Desclou was forced to stop paddling in order to bail. Finally the canoe rounded a smaller island nearby, passing out of sight. Viaud never saw the two men again. Without question, they perished in the ocean soon thereafter.

During the following few days the wind blew from the southeast, making it impossible for the small group to get any oysters. Their only source of food was the wild sorrel, which weakened their stomachs.

Six days elapsed; there was no news from the canoe. Peter felt in his heart that his companions were drowned. That night, as Viaud got up to replenish the bonfire with a large log he had obtained during the afternoon, he suddenly sprang to his feet and shouted over to Madame La Couture, who was almost falling asleep. "What a fool I've been!" he cried. "We have the means of getting off this island whenever we wish! Look at that heavy log. There are many of them around the island. If we put them side by side, lashing them together in some way, we'll have a raft to carry us across to the mainland!"

The next morning those still able to walk began collecting the heavy logs down by the shore. Soon there were enough for a raft that would hold them. Viaud fashioned a mast from a sapling and planned to use a blanket for a sail. His next problem was binding the logs together. He found that the bark of certain trees was pliable and strong, and he cut it from the trees in long, sturdy strips. Reinforced later by pieces of cloth from another blanket, the raft was soon finished and ready for service.

They spent the next few days collecting oysters and all edible material they could find. At last they were ready for the voyage. The journey was planned for the next dawn.

During the night, however, a furious storm broke, not only wrecking and scattering the timbers of their craft, but sinking all their provisions. The four survivors despaired of ever reaching the mainland of Florida, but they knew they must try again. After painfully reconstructing the raft and gathering more supplies for the journey, they were ready once more to drift and sail across to the mainland. It was the 15th of April. Their final blanket, the remainder of their stockings and everything they could possibly spare was used to finish the craft.

Young David La Couture had become ill. When the time came to start, he was found unconscious. Plans for departure were hastily abandoned and all supplies taken ashore from the raft. David, wrapped in the blanket that had been planned for the sail, suddenly awakened and stared at them. Later, when his mother had gone down to the shore to get some food for him, he said to Viaud: "I'm going to die, and the sooner you take my mother off the island the more chance she'll have. Tomorrow I want you to take me away and then tell my mother I have died. You've got to do it, Peter. Promise me."

After much arguing, Viaud agreed to carry out David's plan. The next day, before Madame La Couture awakened, Viaud carried David into the woods until they reached a small, secluded clearing, where he arranged a litter for the boy. Working rapidly, he placed sorrel, water, the edible roots of several trees and a great heap of oysters nearby. Then he bade farewell to David and returned to camp.

Telling Madame La Couture as best he could of the supposed death of her son, Viaud announced that he had buried him in the forest, and that David's last wish was that they should start for the mainland at once.

An hour later Madame La Couture, the slave and Viaud were sailing toward the mainland. In less than twelve hours they landed there. As far as Viaud could estimate, it was April 19, 1766.

They landed on swampy ground. After a search they found an elevated spot, sheltered by leafy trees. Viaud made a fire and all three ate heartily, then fell asleep.

They were awakened in darkness by the noises of wild beasts, evidently close by. The slave fled in terror up the nearest tree, and Madame La Couture followed him. Viaud implored her not to leave the safety of the fire, but she paid no attention. Suddenly, without warning, she found herself trapped in the tree by a bear. Viaud quickly pulled a blazing timber from the campfire and forced the animal away while Madame La Couture scrambled down. When they returned to replenish the burning logs, the bear began to climb the tree after the slave, whose cries intermingled with the roar of the

pursuing bear. Viaud seized several blazing logs and threw
them against the base of the tree. The bear disappeared into
the forest and the frightened slave descended to the ground.

There was no more sleep possible that night. The wild animals continued to surround the camp, howling and roaring
until the coming of dawn sent them away.

The three survivors planned to set out at once for their destination, Fort Saint Marks, which Chief Antonio had indicated
was to the east. They began to walk, but their physical condition did not allow rapid progress. Aware of the coming dangers
of night, the group stopped at sunset to gather a huge amount
of firewood. They arranged a dozen small piles in readiness for
darkness. Next came the problem of food, but there was none
to be found. They did discover water and drank it thirstily.

At night they lighted their fires. No wild animals were heard
until about midnight, when they appeared to be uncomfortably close. There was no attack, however, and the welcome
light of dawn soon arrived.

Still there was no food. In desperation the slave tore off
handfuls of leaves from a tree and devoured them. The others
followed suit, and all three were later seized with terrible
cramps.

Day after day they continued to make slow progress toward
Saint Marks. Finally came the morning of crisis when Viaud
realized they did not have the strength to continue. All three
were delirious with hunger; the mind had become "the slave
of the body," as Viaud later explained. He looked across at the
emaciated body of Madame La Couture, then turned his eyes
on the poor young slave, who was sound asleep. His eyes met
the woman's in what he later declared was perfect understanding. In order to provide food, he would sacrifice the slave.

Unable to stop his disordered mind from acting on this impulse, Peter stepped over to the fire, seized a knotted stick and
approached the sleeping form. Desperately needed food was
his only thought. He brought the club down on the boy's head.

The slave screamed in anguish. Viaud blindly continued his horrible pounding until the lad was dead.

For the next few days both Madame La Couture and Viaud used the remains of the slave to keep alive. Gaining renewed energy from the human meat, they continued to journey toward Fort Saint Marks. What their thoughts were as they made their way through the forest we shall never know.

The traveling was wretched, for they had to struggle through thickets, brambles and thorns hour after hour. At one time they were attacked by literally tens of thousands of mosquitoes and sand flies, which left their bodies swollen and disfigured. Each day they would return to the seashore, catching a few cockles and flounders but, as Viaud said, "Never enough for a meal."

Some time later they could find no food either along the shore or inland, but the roars and cries of the wild animals that night suggested a plan to Viaud. When morning came he set fire to the entire woods. After the flames died down, he found enough burned animals to have palatable food for several days. When they discovered two large dead rattlesnakes, one with fourteen rattles and the other with twenty-one, they were more than happy. Cutting off the heads, they devoured the meat, which tasted delicious to them.

A few days later they came upon an alligator. Killing it, Peter made shoes from its skin and masks to protect their faces from insects. They also ate the flesh, but neither enjoyed it.

Then they reached a swift-moving river they could not ford. Following its bank, they proceeded for two full days before finding and killing a ten-pound land tortoise. As Viaud prepared to cook the tortoise, he discovered that he had lost the vital flint. He could not make a fire!

Viaud believed he had dropped the flint either at the last night's camp or somewhere between the two camps. He started out alone to find it, searching every inch of their path. He soon reached the old camp, but five hours of careful investigation failed to produce the flint. In despair he flung himself on a soft bed of ferns—and touched the metal of the missing flint!

Darkness had descended before Viaud reached Madame La Couture. He could hear the crashing of wild animals as they began their nocturnal wanderings. Viaud soon had a roaring blaze sending sparks up through the tops of the trees. They broiled the tortoise, ate their meal and fell asleep.

Revived next morning by the tortoise meat, they constructed a raft and attempted to pole across the river. The raft struck a tree trunk, however, and they were thrown into the stream. Viaud used the trunk to steady himself while he pulled Madame La Couture to safety. Building a fresh fire, they dried their clothes and ate the rest of the tortoise before sleep overtook them.

The following morning they set out due east. They ran into another great horde of mosquitoes, flies and wasps. Their bodies again began to swell, and Viaud soon began to suffer from a bad fever caused by the insect bites. Madame La Couture was still able to walk.

"Go on and forget me," Viaud declared. "You have a good chance now. I can't get there."

"I will never abandon you," was her answer. Finding and killing another tortoise, she bathed Peter's body in its blood, which seemed to afford him some relief. But that afternoon he grew worse and felt that he would die soon. Madame La Couture had vanished into the underbrush in pursuit of a turkey that had appeared a few feet away.

Suddenly Peter imagined that he could hear the sound of human voices, apparently men in conversation. Afraid that they were savages, he remained quiet for a long time until sure that he recognized English being spoken. When he first attempted to sit up, it was too much for him. Again he tried to raise himself, this time reaching a half-upright position. He crept in the direction of the voices. Suddenly he saw a large boat offshore and began to tremble with excitement. Grabbing a long stick, he tied his tattered clothing to it and placed his cap at the top. Then he waved feebly at the craft, trying to shout but unable to make himself heard. Finally a soldier walked over to the shore side of the ship and noticed him.

"Hello!" the British voice cried. "We've been looking for you!"

Viaud slumped to the ground in a faint. He awakened a short time later to find the strangers pouring tafia down his tortured throat. Madame La Couture appeared at last, carrying the turkey and the turkey's nest. Her joy knew no bounds when she realized they were saved.

The British soldiers were from Fort Saint Marks, out looking for survivors from a shipwreck they knew must have occurred because they had found the dead body of a European on the beach nearby.

By nightfall the next day they were in the vicinity of Fort Saint Marks. But Viaud began to wonder about young David La Couture and if he might still be alive, though it had been nineteen days since they had left him. The soldiers agreed to sail back to the original island with Viaud and Madame La Couture to look for David.

They found the lad, apparently dead. Digging a grave, the soldiers asked Viaud to say a prayer for David. When they leaned over to lift the body into the grave, one of the soldiers gave a cry.

"Wait, men, this boy's still alive!"

When Viaud felt David's chest the heartbeat was noticeable, feeble but steady. Madame La Couture rushed forward and threw herself on the ground beside her son. Restraining her, the others raised the boy tenderly and carried him to the boat. They immediately set sail for Fort Saint Marks and soon arrived.

All three survivors eventually recovered, but the miracle of young David La Couture was discussed for many years by all who knew of it. How a boy, left to die on a lonely island, could live alone for nineteen days was declared one of the mysteries of the century.

It had been eighty-one days from the shipwreck to the arrival of the three survivors at the fort. Two of the company had perished in or near the vessel, two had drowned in the canoe and one had been murdered. The eight seamen left at the camp of the Indians had killed Antonio's mother, sister and nephew in the chief's absence. Five of them had then fled in a canoe. They were never heard from again.

If this were fiction, undoubtedly Madame La Couture and Viaud would have married. But in reality he sailed to Saint Augustine, then traveled to New York and eventually made his way back to France. He never again saw Madame La Couture after he bade her and David farewell at Fort Saint Marks, where she waited for a ship to take her to Louisiana.

In later years Peter Viaud always carried with him a letter written by the commanding officer of Fort Saint Marks, Lieutenant Swettenham, verifying the strange adventures following the unfortunate shipwreck of the *Tiger*.

Whether Peter Viaud and Madame La Couture told their rescuers of their cannibalistic act is a question that remains unanswered. Whether or not they revealed their deed to young David is another enigma. Eventually, however, Peter Viaud did tell the entire story, perhaps at the urging of an anguished conscience.

2

The Unbelievable
Siege of Louisbourg

More than forty years ago, when I was doing research for a lecture series on American coastal defenses, I found a striking illustration of unpreparedness. In 1745 the seemingly impregnable French fortification at Louisburg * on Cape Breton Island fell to New Englanders after a relatively short siege of about two months. At least 2¼ centuries after the siege, I flew over Louisburg and tried to visualize the strange, dramatic episodes that led to the final surrender of the largest artificial stronghold the French ever had in the Western Hemisphere. It was here that an ill-sorted group of American merchants, farmers, country squires and fishermen overcame the well-trained soldiers of the armies of France.

To build the fort, France expended thirty million livres and used her best engineers. Constructed from plans furnished by master bastille designer Marquis Sébastien Vauban, military engineer extraordinary for Louis XIV, the fort took more than twenty-five years to complete.

In 1744, with the outbreak of the Austrian War of Succession, Commander Duquesnal of Louisbourg sent an expedi-

---

* The town's name is *Louisburg,* but the fort itself is spelled *Louisbourg.*

tion against the Nova Scotia town of Canso, which he conquered. He planned to seize Annapolis Royal also, but failed.
His activity aroused not only the English but also the people of
Massachusetts, who rose up in great indignation against him.
Nova Scotia and Maine were under English rule until 1820,
and the colonists resented intervention from the Frenchman.
They were also infuriated that the fort was being used as a
base by French privateers who preyed on New England
fishermen working the Grand Banks.

The leading agitator for revenge was William Vaughan,
owner of successful fishing and lumbering enterprises around
Damariscotta, Maine. Vaughan convinced Governor William
Shirley of the possibility of besieging Louisbourg, and later he
was active in achieving this objective.

One cold January day in 1745, Governor William Shirley
privately communicated with the General Court of Massachusetts regarding the situation between Massachusetts
and Cape Breton Island. Meeting in secret session, he informed the court that he was considering the capture of
France's mighty stronghold, Louisbourg. The plan was first
voted down, but the governor persevered and won approval.

The secrecy of the scheme was violated when one religious
council member prayed too loudly for its success. Devout but
unwise, he explained to the Lord in detail the plans for the
expedition, and soon the entire countryside was aware of the
secret. When the scheme became known, public reaction was
strong against it. Another ballot was then taken in open session. The expedition won by a single vote. (The tying vote was
lost when one member broke his leg hurrying to the council
chamber.)

Governor Shirley, whose enthusiasm for the project was not
lessened by his narrow victory, wrote of his plans to other
colonies as far south as Pennsylvania. The response was amazing. Even faraway Pennsylvania sent supplies. New Hampshire provided five hundred men; Rhode Island voted a sloop;
Connecticut offered 516 men with certain conditions at-

tached; and Massachusetts planned to provide three thousand troops plus the commanding officer of the entire expedition.

The choice of the commander was a problem, however. Not in all New England, according to Governor Wanton of Rhode Island, was there one experienced military officer. William Pepperrell of Kittery, Maine—then part of Massachusetts—was well known as a prosperous trader and so was appointed to lead the expedition. The army, hastily assembled, drilled assiduously for the next few weeks. The troops were composed of outstanding men of each community: country squires, farmers, merchants and shipmasters. In many cases they had left their wives and children to enlist at twenty-five shillings a month.

Finally, when no word of approval or disapproval came from England, Governor Shirley ordained that the expedition should go forward as planned. On March 24, 1745, the fleet of 2070 men and 106 ships sailed from Nantasket Road. The final words of Reverend George Whitefield were *Nil Desperandum Christo Duce (No despair while Christ leads)* which became the motto of the expedition.

There was no reason the expedition should have succeeded. The troops knew nothing of military life or of the conditions they might encounter. They acted for the most part as though they were on a vacation tour. One historian claimed the siege resembled a Harvard commencement in the old days when such activities were not taken too seriously. The audacity of the entire project impressed Benjamin Franklin so unfavorably that he wrote a Boston friend asking several pertinent questions.

An idea of the military caliber of the attacking army can be gleaned from a plan made by one of its enthusiastic New England strategists. It was suggested that two men should be sent out at night to scout the area surrounding Louisbourg's fortifications for the presence of land mines. One soldier was to beat on the ground with a mallet while the other placed his ear against the ground to detect any hollow sound indicating the presence of a mine. If the test was positive, the soldiers were to mark the spot with chalk as a warning to the attacking troops.

The New England regulars had only a few large-size cannon, but they brought a substantial supply of cannonballs. Knowing that the French had cannon, the Americans planned to seize the outlying areas of the fort and then use their ammunition in the captured French cannon. Believe it or not, that is what actually happened.

On Friday, April 5, 1745, the American fleet arrived at Canso, seventy miles across the water from Louisburg. They quickly overcame the small garrison of French soldiers. In Canso the men of New England completed their training for the great undertaking. The English navy also was active, capturing enemy ships and cutting communication lines to Louisburg.

The fleet sailed from Canso for Louisburg on the morning of April 29, intending to arrive at the walls of the great stronghold around nine o'clock at night. The wind fell, however, and it was the following morning before the New Englanders obtained their first glimpse of the Gibraltar of America.

The complete indifference to the arrival of the American fleet by the French soldiers is beyond belief. It is not true, as many claim, that the New Englanders surprised the defenders of Louisbourg. The Frenchmen had known for two months that American forces were planning to capture their stronghold. The mystery is why the landing and the subsequent capture of the outer defenses were not opposed; no one has yet been able to explain it satisfactorily.

The provincial forces made a creditable landing some three miles below the fort. Colonel Vaughan marched four hundred soldiers outside the walls of the mighty citadel and led them in three great cheers, which echoed strangely in the ears of the defenders of Louisbourg. What type of men could these New Englanders be, they thought, to fight their battles with cheers instead of bullets? There was not the slightest opposition to the cheering, so Vaughan paraded his four hundred men over

to the northeast arm of Louisburg Harbor. There he proceeded
to set fire to the naval stores.

The mightiest outlying defense of Louisbourg, known as the
Grand Battery, was about a mile from town. The next day
Colonel Vaughan marched his forces toward the Grand Battery, halting a few hundred yards away. Vaughan sent a
scout—a Cape Cod Indian, brandy bottle in hand—to pretend
that he was drunkenly staggering toward the fort. The Indian
started for the Grand Battery, waving his bottle in the air,
swaying from side to side. Finally he reached the outpost.
There was not a single Frenchman around. The entire Grand
Battery, which had cost the people of France a terrific sum to
build, was empty! It was so strange that Colonel Vaughan
suspected a trick.

To his surprise, Vaughan took possession of the Grand Battery without opposition. He then sent his drummer boy to
unfurl a red undershirt from the top of the flagstaff as an
emblem of the might of New England. Not only had the fort
been deserted, but it was fortified with thirty unmanned cannon, waiting for the New Englanders.

Some cannon were not in firing condition; only a small
number of troops was needed to man those that were. The
remaining idle soldiers decided to hold what amounted to a
Donnybrook Fair in the open ground near the Grand Battery.
Lines were drawn up and measured off for a track meet, and
the men of Boston raced against the men of Providence,
Hartford and Portsmouth. The meets were held to the accom-
paniment of booming guns from the New England forces and
the answering crash of French cannonballs from the main
fort. When the Americans ran short of ammunition, the winners of the foot races were sent chasing after French cannonballs, which were brought back to be used by the Americans.
Other groups were pitching quoits, wrestling or firing their
precious ammunition at bird targets. One squad decided to go
fishing nearby; several of the soldiers who strayed too far were
scalped by the Indians. The whole expedition would have

made excellent material for a Gilbert and Sullivan operetta.

However, the New England gunners knew what they were doing. The first burst from their cannon killed fourteen men at Louisbourg. An artillery precision test between the New Hampshire gunners in the Grand Battery and the defenders of Louisbourg was the highlight of the entire siege. The men from New Hampshire won easily.

On May 20 the mighty French man-of-war *Vigilant*, with forty-six guns and a crew of 560, sailed unsuspectingly into the bay. After a brief but hot exchange, the French surrendered.

Pleased with their progress, the New Englanders set up a battery 1600 yards from the West Gate of the main fort, another battery a thousand yards away to rake the entire town, and a third only a quarter mile from the city itself. This aroused the French forces. They attempted a sortie but were repulsed. Thirty more cannon hidden under water were discovered by scouts. Raised by the Americans from the bottom of the northeast harbor near the lighthouse, they were put in condition and turned against the defenders of Island Battery, one thousand yards away.

An attack against the French at Island Battery was attempted by a whaleboat army. It was driven back, with two hundred American casualties. Pepperrell finally conceived the plan of seizing the lighthouse. The New Englanders climbed the beacon, fired directly down on the battery and captured the island.

Another battery established against the West Gate destroyed the drawbridge. American troops surrounding the entire area prevented reinforcements from reaching Louisbourg by land. In the dead of night, the Americans sent a fireship to burn three French vessels in the harbor. The rest of the fleet, unable to enter the harbor and aid the beleaguered fort, was either captured or fled to the open sea. Finally the Americans so damaged the fortification that the French, after a defense which at first was conspicuous for its complete indifference and later developed into a bitter struggle for survival, surrendered their mighty bastion.

On June 26 Commander Du Chambon of Louisbourg asked for a truce. Two days later, at two o'clock in the afternoon, the British fleet entered the harbor in triumph. At four o'clock the same afternoon, the army marched in by the South Gate. The French soldiers, accorded the full honors of defeated troops, then marched out of the fort in orderly fashion.

Parson Samuel Moody lost no time destroying what he called symbols of idolatry in the Louisburg parish church. He had carried an axe precisely for this purpose all the way from New England. The cross was removed from the chapel and later sent to Harvard College, where it is still pointed out.

During the siege the British officers plundered the Spanish ship *Deliberanza,* taking a million pounds in all. The amount of booty probably angered Pepperrell, who spent ten thousand pounds of his own money to carry out the expedition and received nothing in return. To add insult to injury, he was allegedly charged with the ridiculous theft of the French governor's garters and six silver spoons.

The expedition had its cruel, bitter side. Many did not return from Louisburg. The colonists left to guard their prize the following winter were plagued with pestilence. No less than nine hundred of them died and were laid in shallow graves along the shore. Even today, storms occasionally wash out the skeletons of brave New England men buried there more than two centuries ago.

It was a magnificent feat of American daring. Had it occurred in the days of Chaucer or King Arthur, it would have been immortalized in saga. Why the French permitted it to happen is still a total mystery.

3
_____

Loss of
the Packet *Antelope*

Since childhood I have heard the story of how my grandfather, Captain Joshua N. Rowe, was shipwrecked aboard the clipper ship *Crystal Palace* on the island of Mindanao in the Philippines. He and the others repaired the damage, fought off pirates and then sailed to Macao. They put out again on August 30, 1859, and after a record voyage landed at Plymouth, England, on October 27, 1859.

About three-quarters of a century before, another vessel sailing from Macao to England met disaster on a reef some 500 miles east of the island where Grandfather Rowe was wrecked. Captain Henry Wilson sailed that vessel, the packet *Antelope*, out of Macao on Sunday, July 20, 1783.

Stormy weather beset them until Friday, August 8, when the skies began to moderate, giving way to a relatively calm Saturday. Since it was then possible to throw open the ship's ports and dry out the cabin, the spirits of those aboard rose and all looked forward to better sailing conditions.

Unfortunately, heavy rain and a thunderstorm struck early Sunday morning. Suddenly breakers were reported dead ahead. Before any orders could be given, the *Antelope* struck heavily. Complete confusion ensued. The ship bilged within the hour and filled with water to the lower deck hatchways.

With his air of confidence and decision, Captain Wilson brought order out of chaos. Soon he had the gunpowder and small arms secured, the bread safe on deck and many of the other provisions protected from the water. He ordered the mizzenmast cut away to prevent excessive heeling, then gave directions for the main topmast and fore-topmast to be removed and the main and foreyards to be lowered. The boats were hoisted out and filled with provisions. Plans were made to abandon the wreck hurriedly if necessary.

The wait for dawn began. Two glasses of wine and several biscuits were doled out to each person. Everything possible was done to allay the fears of the anxious passengers.

At daybreak they discovered a small island about ten miles to the south and later made out several other islands to the east. Captain Wilson chose the smaller but nearest island to the south for their destination. The boats left the ship with orders to proceed there.

Those who remained aboard the wreck started building a raft in case the *Antelope* began to break up. In the afternoon when the boats returned, the sailors reported that five men had been left with the stores on the island and that no natives had appeared. This good news caused the captain to order another glass of wine and more biscuit for all hands, but the loss of a man overboard at this time stopped the celebrating.

Finally the raft was finished. The men loaded it with a great number of stores and then completely stocked the jolly boat and the pinnace.

The latter now started out towing the raft, with the jolly boat going on ahead. At times the pinnace crew could not even see the raft because of the giant waves. Eventually they reached the island and unloaded the cargo.

During the next few days the captain and several others attempted to free the ship. When a great wind blew up and it appeared that the packet would go to pieces, those at the wreck were able to return safely to the island.

At about eight o'clock the next morning, two canoes were observed approaching the island. Tom Rose from the Malayan Peninsula was chosen to negotiate with the natives in the canoes when they reached shore. As soon as they were within hailing distance, Tom began. The usual questions were asked concerning the presence of the white men on the island. Satisfactory explanations were given. Finally Tom called to Captain Wilson, who strode down the beach and waded into the sea waist-deep to greet the strangers.

Among the eight natives were two princes, brothers of the king of their tribe on neighboring Ternate Island. The men explained that the masts of the *Antelope* had been seen by fellow islanders fishing from a canoe.

The whites, still very suspicious of the natives, tried to conceal their feelings as they sat down to breakfast with them shortly afterward. During the meal the men talked about the area where the *Antelope* was wrecked. The Palau (or Pelew) Islands, and especially Oroolong where they had been cast away, are about 500 miles due east of Mindanao Island in the Philippines. They were first called the Palos Islands by the Spaniards, who believed the tall palm trees resembled masts of ships when seen from a distance.

The native men who sat around the breakfast table were copper-colored, admirably proportioned and quite naked. Their thighs were much blacker than the rest of their bodies because of tattooing. The chief, or prince, carried a small basket containing betel nuts and chinam, which is coral burned to lime. The natives would sprinkle the leaf of the betel nut with the lime powder and then chew the leaves, forcing the red juice between their already blackened teeth.

Finally the natives decided that they had stayed long enough at the island. They requested Captain Wilson to appoint one person to return with them for a visit of respect to their king. Wilson deliberated a few minutes about this awkward predicament, then chose his brother, Matthias Wilson. He told Matthias to ask for protection and also permission to build a vessel in which they could sail back to their own country. Captain Wilson sent the king a package of presents—broadcloth, a canister of tea, a jar of sugar candy and a bottle of rusk.

It was also agreed that the king's brother, Prince Raa Kook, and three other natives would remain with the white men and help them. The prince soon found a fine well of water on another part of the island. Then he went down to the beach with his companions and the white men to say good-by to the natives in the two canoes as they started for the island where the king lived.

Meanwhile, other natives had been plundering the wreck, as Captain Wilson found out to his disappointment. He was especially concerned when he discovered that the medicine chest had been ransacked, the costly and vital fluids emptied because the natives coveted the bottles. When the captain told Prince Kook about it, the prince was enraged and promised vehemently to kill any natives caught plundering the ship in the future.

There was a large store of choice wines and liquors on board the *Antelope*. Captain Wilson knew the relative strength of such intoxicants on the empty stomachs of his men. Therefore he suggested to the other officers that they go aboard the packet and stave in every one of the scores of liquor casks. The task was carried out at once, not one man imbibing in even a farewell glass.

On the morning of August 14 two canoes arrived, bringing Arra Kooker, the king's other brother, and one of the king's sons. A third canoe, so the natives claimed, had been delayed by the wind. Aboard that craft was Matthias Wilson. Some of the white men wondered whether he was being forcibly detained.

After introductions, everyone went over to the wreck. There they found twenty native canoes, which Raa Kook dispersed at once.

Returning to the island, Arra Kooker amused the others by

telling of Matthias Wilson's concern while visiting the king, explaining by facetious mimicry the apprehension Matthias had shown when he was the only white man in the center of hundreds of savages. Shortly afterward the canoe was sighted with Matthias aboard, and Captain Wilson heaved a sigh of relief.

Matthias told of his experiences while visiting the king. He had given the presents to the monarch in a respectful manner, and they were graciously accepted. Then Matthias had been allowed to mingle with the scores of people in the little enclosure where the king received him. The natives crowded around the white man, believing his clothing was part of him; they all were completely naked and had never seen a clothed man before. When Matthias took off his hat, unbuttoned his waistcoat and removed his shoes, their wonderment knew no bounds.

With the approach of evening, Matthias explained, he had been greatly concerned when two groups of natives lit large bonfires, one on each side of him. He wondered if they were about to roast him alive. But the king, noticing his apprehension, explained that the fires were to keep Matthias warm during the long tropical night. Matthias fell asleep shortly afterward, to be awakened by the bright sun shining in the east.

For breakfast he was given yams, coconuts and sweetmeats. A wind of great strength had come up, and the king decided that Matthias should wait till the following day before returning to Captain Wilson. The next morning two canoes were sent out ahead. A few hours later, in still calmer weather, a third canoe with a picked crew transported Matthias back to Oroolong, the island near which they had been wrecked.

Captain Wilson was highly pleased. His brother's account made him confident that the natives were going to remain friendly. The king showed no objections to the white men building a craft in which to sail for home, and the captain at once started making plans to construct a vessel large enough to transport them all.

Meanwhile, certain formalities had to be observed. The king had promised Matthias that he would soon visit the white men's settlement. When a number of canoes were seen approaching early the next morning, Arra excitedly told Wilson that the great king of the Pelew Islands was in one of the canoes.

Soon an impressive marine procession entered the little harbor. The king's canoe was easily identified as it proceeded with two other craft on each side, making a dramatic spectacle approaching the beach side by side. Trained natives pulled their paddles high out of the water, each flourish in perfect coordination. As the paddlers neared the beach, four natives in each canoe brought forward their conches and at a given signal blew the shells like trumpets to announce the arrival of His Majesty King Abba Thulle.

Captain Wilson, instructed by Arra Kooker, went down to the low-water mark on shore to welcome the king. He was brought out into the shallow water to His Majesty, who was seated on an impromptu throne built in the center of the canoe. Stepping aboard, Captain Wilson and the king embraced each other. The monarch now stated that he was ready to go ashore. Captain Wilson was carried to the beach by the natives, but the naked king walked ashore himself. Because he refused to enter any of the tents that had been set up on the island, the white people spread a sail on the ground and escorted him to the center of it.

After Captain Wilson introduced the other officers of his crew, the king asked him to identify his badge of supremacy. At a loss for an answer, Captain Wilson was aided by Chief Mate Benger, who surreptitiously slipped a beautiful gold ring into Wilson's hand. Wilson slipped it on his own finger as he stepped forward to the king.

"Your Majesty," he began, "this is typical of my symbol of authority." He pulled the ring from his finger and gave it to the king, who tried it on and was very pleased at the token of leadership Captain Wilson had shown him.

The captain now reintroduced his chief mate. The king called him "Kickary Rupack," which meant "Little Chief."

The native leader was impressed with the ship's grindstone, which had been placed on a block on shore. He took hold of the handle and turned it. Then his attention went to the muskets, and he asked questions about them. Captain Wilson promised to arrange a demonstration. In a short time the sailors conducted a drill on the lowtide beach, which they concluded by aiming their guns at a saluting angle and firing three volleys. The king and his followers were overwhelmed by the exhibition.

To press his advantage, Captain Wilson asked the chief mate to put on a special demonstration of shooting. A fowl was released to strut along the beach, and "Kickary Rupack" shot him with one blast. The natives rushed to the remains, examined them and were again dumbfounded.

That night the savages sang their customary songs, which some of the white men misinterpreted as preliminaries to a massacre. A scuffle started that might have led to serious trouble, but the king and Captain Wilson soon quieted both sides. After a few English songs were sung, the remainder of the night was spent in sleep.

Then came the first efforts to build a ship from the wreckage of the *Antelope*. The natives were anxious to watch the proceedings. But the English, not knowing how far to trust the savages, had concealed many tools and weapons from them. To the consternation of all, a native discovered one of the cutlasses, demanded it and finally stalked off in triumph as the white men let him have it. Seeing the man with the cutlass, Raa Kook angrily took it away and gave it back to Wilson. The incident caused some unpleasantness, for Captain Wilson had lost face by giving the cutlass to an inferior member of the tribe. Native protocol dictated that only royalty receive gifts of such importance.

A neighboring tribe at Artingall Island had bothered the king a short time before arrival of the white men. Abba Thulle thought a show of strength would be timely. It was arranged that five Englishmen armed with their magic guns would accompany the native warriors to the offenders' island. In the battle that followed, the neighboring tribe was first terrorized and then overwhelmed by the firearms. On September 4 Captain Wilson gave permission for a second demonstration, during which ten of his men were to fight on the side of Abba Thulle's warriors. This second battle with the king's enemies at Artingall Island also ended successfully, and the king returned to his own island well pleased.

Meanwhile, building of the vessel progressed. While the framework was being erected, Abba Thulle appeared with news that the chief minister at Artingall was suing for peace. Realizing the importance of the guns in obtaining the victory, the king requested that when Wilson completed his ship and sailed away, he leave behind ten muskets for safety. Wilson tentatively compromised at five muskets, and there the matter ended for the time being.

The vessel was breamed by October 27. The outside caulking was completed, but there was neither pitch nor tar to pay her with. The sailors burned coral into lime, mixed it with grease and used it as a substitute.

On November 6 Captain Wilson sent the jolly boat across to Pelew, requesting the honor of the king's presence within a few days. It was also announced that seaman Madan Blanchard was so impressed with native life that he was anxious to stay behind. When the king arrived at Oroolong, Wilson told him Blanchard would remain to instruct the natives in firing muskets and using the iron tools Captain Wilson planned to leave with them. The king consented gladly.

On November 9, a Sunday, in the presence of the King of Pelew, the new vessel was launched and named *Oroolong*. She appeared neat and trim as she lay at anchor in the cove.

After a happy breakfast the men began carrying aboard all their possessions. Next the ship was hauled into the basin, where there was about twenty feet of water, and the remainder of the cargo was loaded, except for the heavy guns and other weighty objects.

A short time later Abba Thulle told Wilson the local rupacks had decided to make him an honorary prince of the first rank. Giving him a circular bone standing for the rank of prince, the king said: "You are now invested with our highest mark of honor, and this bone, the signal of it, you will carefully keep as bright as possible, rubbing it every day. This high mark of dignity must always be valiantly defended, nor suffered to be wrested from you but with your life."

Then came the great surprise. Abba Thulle informed Captain Wilson that he was sending his second son, Prince Lee Boo, back with Captain Wilson so that he would get a thorough education and eventually return with knowledge he could impart to his countrymen. Overcome by the news, Captain Wilson agreed gladly and ordered quarters prepared on the *Oroolong.*

Among the ship's company was a huge Newfoundland dog that had delighted Arra Kooker. The prince was overjoyed when the captain gave him the prized pet. Arra Kooker planned to build a huge craft on the ship's ways, which Captain Wilson left on the beach.

A final act was to hoist an English pennant on a tree near the cove and put up a copper plate on the trunk of the tree with the following inscription:

THE HONORABLE ENGLISH
EAST INDIA COMPANY'S SHIP THE ANTELOPE
HENRY WILSON COMMANDER
WAS LOST UPON THE REEF NORTH OF THIS
ISLAND
IN THE NIGHT
BETWEEN THE 9TH AND 10TH OF AUGUST
WHO HERE BUILT A VESSEL
AND SAILED FROM HENCE
THE 12TH OF NOVEMBER, 1783

Now came an unpleasant discussion concerning firearms. When Abba Thulle renewed his request for the ten muskets, he was refused. Quick to resent this attitude, the king spoke out frankly. "Why should you distrust me? I have never refused you my confidence. If my intentions had been hostile, you would have known it long ago, being entirely in my power. And yet, at the very last, you suspect me of bad designs!"

His straightforward manner embarrassed the white men. Without further hesitation they gave the king five muskets, five cutlasses and almost a full barrel of gunpowder, with flint and ball in proportion. In this way peace and goodwill were restored, and Abba Thulle soon forgot their unkind suspicions.

During the evening Prince Lee Boo arrived from Pelew with his elder brother, and Abba Thulle presented him to all the officers. The night was spent ashore, with the king giving advice to his son.

Early Wednesday morning a signal gun was sounded from the *Oroolong* and camp ashore was broken at once. All persons left the island, the white men not to return.

As soon as farewells were made, the *Oroolong* hoisted sail and proceeded to a position outside the reef, where guns and other equipment were loaded aboard. Finally all was in readiness for the long trip back to civilization.

The king then directed that his canoe be brought alongside. Going aboard, he gave his son a farewell blessing, spoke briefly to the captain and prepared to leave the vessel. Fruit and food of all kinds were now carried aboard from the native canoes. Then Captain Wilson ordered a package carried forward for the king. It contained a brace of pistols and a cartouche box of cartridges.

Now came the final moment. King Abba Thulle stepped forward and began to speak slowly. "You are happy because you are going. I am happy because you are happy, but still very unhappy to see you going away."

The captain was so overcome that he was momentarily unable to answer, and the king was equally moved. Finally, pointing to his heart, Abba Thulle stepped over the side into his waiting canoe, which was a signal for a conch salute.

The *Oroolong* rapidly progressed out of the harbor, leaving the natives far behind within an hour. It was November 12 that the ship's company thus terminated their enforced stay at the island, which began on August 10.

Aboard the *Oroolong* Prince Lee Boo was placed in the care of Mr. Sharp, the surgeon, who taught him the fundamentals of dress and behavior during the voyage to China. On November 25 the crew sighted the Bashee Islands. This greatly pleased the prince, who was happy to see land once more. The next day Formosa was in sight, bearing northeast, and on the 29th the ship anchored near the high land called the Asses' Ears, arriving at Macao one day later. The Portuguese governor visited the captain and told him the war that had been going on was over, and peace had been established in Europe. A message was forwarded to Canton explaining what had happened to the *Antelope*.

Lee Boo was taken to visit the home of Mr. McIntyre, a friend of Captain Wilson. When the prince saw his image in a large mirror, he was amazed, supposing it to be someone else looking at him. This and other wonders of civilization kept him at a constant pitch of excitement. Arrangements were later made for Captain Wilson, Lee Boo and the officers to embark from Whampoa aboard the *Walpole,* leaving Chief Mate Benger to take over the *Oroolong* and sell her.

The crew was paid off with funds forwarded from Canton, and the next day the *Walpole* sailed away. On July 14, 1784, after an uneventful journey, the *Walpole* put into Portsmouth, England, her long trip ended.

Back in the Pelew Islands, the king had been told on the day Captain Wilson departed that it would be at least thirty moons, and possibly six more, before his son returned. The king had then knotted thirty knots into a rope, left a little space and knotted six more.

But Prince Lee Boo never returned to his father. About six

months after he arrived in England, he caught the dread smallpox disease and died. He is buried in Rotherheathe Cemetery, where a magnificent tomb was erected to his memory by the East India Company. The stone on the tomb reads:

To the memory of
PRINCE LEE BOO
A native of the Pelew, or Palos Islands
and Son to Abba Thulle, Rupack or King
of the Island Coorooraa:
Who departed this life on the 27th of December, 1784,
Aged 20 Years
This stone is inscribed
by the Honorable United East India Company
as a Testimony of esteem for the humane and kind
Treatment afforded by his Father to the crew of
their ship, the ANTELOPE, Captain Wilson,
which was wrecked off that Island
In the night of the 9th of August, 1783.

Stop, Reader, stop—let NATURE claim a Tear—
A Prince of Mine, Lee Boo, lies bury'd here.

4

The Polar Crusoe

On my first visit to Scotland in 1943 I took a brief walk around Aberdeen, where my natural tendencies took me to a bookshop. I soon discovered a score of fascinating story possibilities, one of which I found impossible to leave. Because I was about to sail on what was then the world's largest ship, the *Queen Elizabeth,* a few speedy notes were all I could manage that day. Later, as I browsed deeper and deeper, I could not believe the tale. But subsequent research has won me over.

In 1757 a vessel named the *Anne Forbes* left the port of Aberdeen, Scotland, for the Greenland whaling grounds. On board, as a seaman, was a lad by the name of Bruce Gordon. The captain was Emmet Hughes, an Englishman with the reputation of being a rash, obstinate drunkard.

On her way to the whaling area the ship had fine weather and an open sea at first. Then one day a girdle of ice was sighted, about thirty miles broad. The whaler sailed between this obstruction and Iceland. Reaching a latitude of 70 degrees North, she came upon some gigantic whales journeying rapidly northward. The crew captured one and then continued on their route for two weeks. Although the mate, an old experienced sailor, repeatedly told the captain of the danger of penetrating so far into the Polar seas, Captain Hughes only laughed and declared that they were now at the Pole and could sail to China as easily as to Spain.

There were plenty of whales, and they harpooned so many they loaded the vessel. Despite this rich haul, Captain Hughes ignored the approach of colder weather and refused to head south. He was drinking heavily, bragging about his great feat of discovering the North Pole. For the next few days the mate persistently pointed out to his commanding officer several of the worst ice floes in the vicinity, which would certainly imprison the ship if the wind should rise from that direction. Captain Hughes berated him for being a nuisance.

One afternoon the mate noticed that the vessel had entered a strong current and was drifting northward. Realizing that the *Forbes* was being swept rapidly toward danger, the mate again spoke to the captain. This time he was sobered by the situation and ordered all sails set. Taking the sun's altitude, he suddenly became terribly worried and commanded the course to be set due south.

The current was strong against them, with a light breeze on the starboard bow. The ice soon forced itself against the ship on all sides. Even worse, a whitish fog began to cover them. Staying on deck, the captain barked orders with an impatience born of fear.

Despite all their efforts the ship became completely surrounded by the relentless floes, which were still sufficiently loose to allow slow progress toward the southwest under short sail. The *Forbes* passed what the crew took to be a huge iceberg but the captain said was an island, "one of the Seven Sisters" off the coast of Spitsbergen.

After struggling on for twenty-four hours more they noticed another, apparently endless field of ice before them. The mate knew that the moment the two packs collided the ship would be crushed. Just before that occurred he ordered Bruce Gordon up to the masthead.

Within a short time the masts and the bulwarks of the *Anne Forbes* shattered under the terrific impact. The ship went over on her beam ends, throwing Bruce from the mast onto one of the fields of ice. The *Forbes* went down in less than thirty minutes, taking everyone except young Bruce Gordon.

The very next day, as a result of peculiar forces at work below the surface, the vessel rose again, capsized with keel uppermost and became imbedded in the frozen wastes.

So it was that Bruce found himself alone on a field of floating ice, far out on the great Polar ocean, without food or shelter. He happened to have a small Old Testament in his pocket, which his mother had given him when he first went to sea. From this he derived his sole consolation.

He saw at once that his only chance of survival lay in trying to reach the hulk of the wreck. The broken ice had been pushed up in heaps, and there were great gulfs between the floes that had to be crossed. But Bruce was determined to reach the ship—or perish in the attempt.

The way was perilous. After climbing over mountains of ice as firm as rocks, he came to other areas with the consistency of froth, and there he slid into water over his head. The ice was so slippery at times that he could get no hold. He knew that if he went down gradually into the soft spots he was gone. Thus, whenever he found that he was beginning to sink, he jumped in bodily to keep his momentum and managed to spring to a firmer foothold. At length, as he wondered how he could keep up his unequal flight, he reached a broken boat mast. With this for support he finally made his way to the wreck. He was completely exhausted.

The keel of the *Forbes* was uppermost, and there was no way to get inside. He had nothing to dig with save the splinter of mast. The hulk, above the ice, seemed undamaged but impenetrable.

He was terribly thirsty, but all the surrounding ice he tasted was salty. Nearly worn out from his efforts, Bruce noticed not far from him, beyond a level plain of ice, a tremendous berg that he took for a mountain. Hastening toward it, he found to his relief that the ice was fresh, not salty. This was an unexpected blessing, and he knelt and thanked God. Committing himself to His mercy and protection, he broke off sections of ice and ate them until he could stomach no more.

Although his thirst had been satisfied, the pangs of hunger were increasing. He started once more toward the wreck to search for something to eat. Among other things, he found a small boat hook used for the yawl and a harpoon fastened to a part of the shattered longboat. Returning to the hulk with difficulty, he was able to reach the cabin window and force entrance. The cabin was full of ice, with everything turned upside down.

Bruce made his way to the bread locker, broke it open and savored some biscuits. He thought he had never tasted anything so delicious. He ate and ate until he again became thirsty. Fighting through the rubble in the cabin, he reached the captain's secret store closet and broke it open in hopes of getting something stronger than ice water to drink. But every bottle was either empty or smashed.

He located knives and forks, a corkscrew and many other implements that might prove valuable. At length, below all the rubbish, he came upon an entire unbroken cask of spirits. The corkscrew was instantly applied, out flew the bung and down went his nose to the hole. It was either rum or brandy—he believed it was a mixture of the two. Taking the tube of the old ship bellows, he put in the wide end and sucked the small one. Never having tasted anything so strong before, he was little aware of its potency and was soon overcome. He fell fast asleep beside the cask.

Bruce awoke after sleeping for a considerable time, his body so numb that he was unable to get up. He turned again and again to the contents of the barrel.

At length he heard what to his amazement sounded like a great number of people muttering outside the vessel. Weak and tipsy from the liquor he had consumed, Bruce became frightened. His fright turned to terror when he thought he heard somebody enter the cabin through the hole he had made in the stern, followed by the sound of munching at the biscuits.

Vitalized by his fear, he cautiously opened the door of the closet where he had slept. In his delirium he saw what he first believed was a naked woman escaping from the cabin window. He was at least sure that he saw her bare feet and toes. Seizing a boat hook in one hand and a harpoon in the other, he went cautiously to the entrance hole.

Looking out, he saw several white polar bears prowling around the ship, all busily digging and eating. He was amazed at the holes the powerful beasts had clawed in the ice in order to prey on the blubber stored in the ship. They were also attacking the bodies of Bruce's unfortunate companions. Two bears within twelve yards of him were tearing at the corpse of his late captain, which he recognized from the shreds of clothes strewn about.

In an effort to drive the creatures away, Bruce took a speaking-trumpet and shouted through it with all his might, "Avast, ye lubbers!" They sprang up on their hind feet, standing as straight as humans. They were sleek and plump, and one appeared to be at least ten feet high. After staring about them for a time, the bears resumed their gruesome feast.

Bruce tried to frighten them with various kinds of sound. Instead of fleeing, they began to draw nearer to him. Frightened, he barricaded his entrance by fitting a large fire grate into it. He then used oakum to lash knives, forks and other sharp instruments to the grate, facing their points outward.

Thinking he was safe, he retired to the closet and swallowed a tankard of brandy. Then he took the hard, frozen blankets from the cabin bunks and made himself a couch. Locking the door on the inside, he climbed on his bed and was soon asleep. He was not disturbed again by the animals during his slumber.

The long Arctic night was setting in. The bears kept prowling about, but in a more listless manner than before, as if they were well fed. Bruce ate a good amount of salt biscuit; hoar-frost, which lay nearly two inches thick, satisfied his thirst. To warm himself he had recourse to the brandy, which usually set him sleeping for twenty-four hours, sometimes even longer.

Bruce guessed he was somewhere in the middle of the sea between Greenland and the North Cape. With ample spirits and provisions within the wreck—if he could get at them—he believed he could winter on the ice. But to do this he would have to make his way both into the hold and the forecastle, where there were coal and important stores. It would be neces-sary to reach the door, then work himself between the deck and the solid ice below. The fact that everything was upside down added to his difficulties. He spent many a hard day's labor making little progress. When at length he had hacked his way to the hold, Bruce found the whole weight of the cargo lying above it. At first he could not move it.

In the course of his efforts, he discovered the captain's wardrobe, with plenty of shirts and clothes, every article steeped in salt water and frozen. He also found shaving uten-sils, flint and materials for lighting his pipe.

Finally he reached the coal bin. It contained a moderate amount of large pieces of coal, with an old axe for breaking them into smaller fragments. From the rubbish of a boat that had been fastened on deck, he pulled out a squaresail, some smaller canvas, a good hatchet and many other useful articles.

Fire was now the only thing he needed. With it he could melt the ice, cook his food and dry his clothes. Although he had all the materials, without a chimney or smoke vent he could not start a blaze. After various experiments, he at length succeeded in carrying a flue up to the heel of the keel, and found it worked out admirably.

The Arctic winter had set in. No more did he hear the calls of swans and geese journeying southward. A few bears occa-sionally prowled about, but he seldom went outside. He stuffed snow up the entrance he had hacked out, and he fixed a piece of cable to a door so he could close or open it with a minimum of effort.

During the middle of one night when a great Arctic blizzard was raging, Bruce was awakened by a noise outside his cabin. He was frightened beyond measure. The sound continued. Then something came to his closet door and bumped against it. He held his breath. A creature attempted to force open the door but failed. By this time Bruce was on his feet brandishing the large carving knife he always kept beside him. Presently the intruder went away and began to attack the biscuits.

What appeared to be the sound of crunching teeth led Bruce to believe that the unwanted visitor was a polar bear. He struck a light, flung open the door and bolted out, armed with the torch in his left hand and the long sharp knife in his right. His guess had been correct. The flame frightened the creature, who tried to dash out the door with such speed that it stuck fast. Bruce ran forward and gave the animal two deadly stabs in the heart. Blood cascaded across the cabin, and very soon the brute was dead.

The carcass became stiff and began to freeze. Bruce pulled and strained until he had the beast inside the cabin. It proved to be a huge female with "milk in her dug," indicating she had been nursing recently. Bruce skinned her with great difficulty, sliced the flesh into neat square pieces and spread it on the ice to freeze. He figured that he had no less than a hundredweight of good, wholesome, fresh meat. He then cleared out the cabin and washed it with hot water; when the floor had dried, he spread the bear's skin for a carpet. After swallowing some hot punch, he once more retired to bed.

On awakening, he heard another familiar noise at the door, a plaintive grumbling. Cautiously he opened the entrance. Outside, a female polar bear cub, apparently dying of hunger, raised its forefeet as if entreating to be taken in. He helped the small creature inside, and when she found her mother's skin she seemed to utter a bleat of joy. The cub went round and round licking the skin with great fondness, looking for the milk she could no longer get from her mother.

At length the animal seemed to understand that a terrible change had taken place in her mother's body. The baby curled herself on the fur in an attitude of almost human grief. Feeling sorry for the cub, Bruce offered her some biscuit. She accepted the first piece shyly, then ate the rest so voraciously Bruce was afraid she would choke.

He recollected that there were heaps of frozen blubber lying on the ice that he had cleared below the deck of the hold. He crept away with his coal axe and a light, and brought some large pieces into the cabin. These he broke into small bits to feed the cub, patting her and speaking kindly, calling her Nancy after the only girl he ever loved. She licked his hand in return. He was ecstatic at having found a live companion. The cub fell asleep on her mother's skin and did not awaken for three days.

In the meantime Bruce was not idle. On the floor of the forecastle was a trapdoor communicating with the bilge water, into which the crew had emptied foul water without being obliged to run up constantly to the ship's side. There was likewise a trapdoor in the cabin, but that was carpeted and thus seldom opened. On pushing aside the latch of that trapdoor, which he did easily with a table knife, the door fell toward him since the deck was his ceiling.

He entered this hatch hole and discovered himself at the keel of the vessel, among the pig iron. He had a free passage into the hold, where he found more coal and additional casks of fresh water—or, rather, fresh ice—as well as the carcasses of five or six whales. He had meat for the bear cub for years to come, plus plenty of blubber to burn. The forecastle's larder yielded a large barrel half full of beef, and another more than half full of pork. There was also bacon, mutton and deer hams, and about half a cask of Highland whiskey.

He returned to the cabin in a happy mood, taking with him a good piece of solid meat, pipes, snuff and tobacco, all of which he had found nicely packed up in boxes. He tried to awaken

Nancy but in vain; only by holding burning tobacco to her nose, which made her sneeze violently, could she be prevailed upon to open her eyes.

He fed her, and her eyes lighted up. As she weighed only about forty-five pounds, he carried her into his closet and closed the door, but she would not settle down away from the skin of her mother. At last he took the mother's skin into his closet and spread it above his blankets, after which she lay down upon it, uttering the same plaintive sounds as before.

By degrees he taught Nancy to follow him in and out of the wreck. She was never weary of rolling in the snow, often scraping her claws frantically at the ice as if longing to get into the sea. She continued to thrive and soon was as plump as a calf.

She never once showed the least disposition toward anger or surliness, but seemed to consider Bruce a friend of her own species. As the months went by she answered to her name and came at his bidding. When they walked out upon the ice, Bruce dressed in his late captain's holiday clothes, he would take her paw within his arm to teach her to walk upright. He often laughed heartily at the figure they cut. She tried to imitate him in everything, including laughing. Her laugh was irresistible, with the half-closed eyes, a grin and a neigh resembling that of a wild horse.

At length the sun made its appearance above the southern horizon. Every day Bruce worked to cut a regular flight of steps to the top of a giant iceberg near the ship, which would serve as an observation post. He finally finished the rough stairway to the peak of this huge mountain of solid ice, winding it around the innumerable creeks and ravines that went far down into the body of the berg.

The Arctic spring arrived. The swans came north over his head, their weird cries piercing day and night. This, he thought, boded evil for him, for it told him plainly that the Polar seas beyond this great field of ice were open. If the ice

broke up, he was sure to be carried northward among unknown seas and frozen coasts. To prevent such a catastrophe,
he would have to start out in search of land. But he did not
know in what direction to seek either continent or island.

He still had ample food as well as a fowling piece, and he
had dried out a box of gunpowder. Bruce climbed the iceberg
almost every day. At length he resolved to dig a cavern, believing it impossible that the iceberg could melt or sink. He hol-
lowed out several comfortable apartments. One had a chimney
he fashioned with a bar of pig iron. Here he stored part of his
provisions, spirits and other supplies. He resolved to trust himself to the iceberg if he saw the ice breaking up, and leave the
rest to Providence.

For about two months he spent all his waking hours on top
of this ice mountain with Nancy, who was always at his heels.
One morning, which judging by the height and heat of the
sun must have been about midsummer, he looked out from his
observation peak and saw that the whole sea northward was
clear of ice to within a mile of him. At the same time there was
a strong current running in that direction. Everything remained as usual for several days, with Bruce and his cub
staying in one of the chambers he had cut in the iceberg.

He was awakened from a sound sleep one night by a totter-
ing motion of the iceberg. The movement ceased in a minute,
by which time he was up and out on the platform at the top.
He saw that the berg had twisted a small degree to the west
and had separated from the great field of ice on the east, leaving an opening "about a bowsprit over." The wreck remained
on his side of the gap, and he hastened down from the
mountain to see how matters stood there.

The sea in the new opening was as bright as a mirror. As
soon as Nancy saw the water she rushed into it, vanishing
below the ice for so long that Bruce feared for her safety. She
appeared at length with a fish in her mouth, something like a
large herring. He was happy to get fresh fish and caressed her

for it; away she rushed again to the opening. Whenever she dived she brought up a fish, and every day thereafter she kept him well supplied.

Realizing that it was a strong foundation on which the wreck rested, he again began sleeping in his old berth in the cabin closet. One morning when he arose, the ice bordering the beautiful crystal gap of water was gone. They had set off on another Polar voyage, leaving the vast field of ice behind. As far as the eye could see, all was again water.

Lazy walruses rested and rolled on the ledges of the ice mountain. Seals would also have congregated on it had it not been for Nancy, who carried on perpetual and bloody warfare with them.

Bruce must have traversed the Polar seas for at least six months more without ever knowing where he was. Several times he saw mountains. Once he observed a headland or island straight before him. Anxious to see what kind of country it was, he went to the topmost point of the iceberg to watch.

He was so near land that he saw a human being, a woman he thought, moving about on the shore and staring at the floating mountain. He put his two hands to his mouth and hailed the stranger with all the strength of his lungs. But before he could establish real contact, the bear sent forth such a vibrating roar that the native was frightened and vanished among the rocks.

The iceberg, including the attached ledge of ice on which the hulk of the *Anne Forbes* rested, was moved by different currents and driven from one direction to another in that vast Polar sea. At length the fogs returned to cover the face of the ocean. The sun neared the horizon, and from that time forth Bruce saw no more around him—neither sun, moon nor stars—but journeyed on he knew not where. Unless he was busy cleaning the fish Nancy caught, he either dozed, read his Bible (most of which he learned by heart) or amused himself with the antics of his companion. Though he often slept in his ice cave in summer, he moved into his old cabin in the wreck as winter approached.

One day he was frightened when he heard a great rushing noise like a tempest. It continued for some time, although he could perceive no change in the ocean. He decided to walk around the vast mountain of ice, as far as he could go. By the time he was halfway, the mystery was solved.

The new ice had commenced, and the irresistible mass of his frozen island borne along by a strong undercurrent was breaking it up with tremendous violence. The ice continued to roll up before the mountain, and was heaped against it to such a height that finally the berg became fixed and the noise ended.

An intense frost set in one night. The fog cleared away, the stars appeared in the zenith and a beautiful blue twilight sky fringed the horizon. Bruce went to the top of the mountain to look around. Suddenly he was sure that he saw land dead ahead.

While contemplating the scene with disbelief, the report of a gun reached his ears. It sounded like a signal from a ship not many miles away. He hastened from the height, seized his fowling piece and again climbed the peak, where he fired the weapon. After his third shot a report was returned with a roar louder than before. He tried as best he could to imitate the signal of distress. After his signal had been answered, he judged that there was no time to be lost. Hastening down once more, he packed some powder and shot, food and a bottle of spirits and hurried off in the direction from which he thought the sounds came and the land lay.

When he had traveled sixteen to twenty miles, calculated by the length of time he took, he suddenly noticed the bear cub greatly interested in something a long distance to the right. He turned in that direction, and to his astonishment found traces of a company of thirty or forty men, all journeying on the same path straight for land. Thus encouraged, he continued walking for many miles. Nancy, meanwhile, had run off and left him. Straining his eyes, he perceived on high ground that must mark the shore a number of white bears—all coming toward him!

He dared not run for fear of being pursued by the whole band and torn to pieces. Since it also seemed dangerous to advance, he squatted down on the ice and "wished himself under it." The animals had discovered him, however, and they all came toward him. Then he sprang to his feet and ran, without looking back. A noise coming nearer and nearer compelled him to glance over his shoulder, and he perceived two bears in close pursuit.

Terrified, he flung away his provisions, keeping only his loaded gun and his long dirk. The two creatures paused when they came to his supplies and soon devoured the food. Bruce recognized the smaller bear as Nancy. Evidently the larger bear, a male, had become interested in her and had followed her. Realizing the other bear could easily kill Bruce, she scampered in the opposite direction over the icy wastes to lead the bear away.

Bruce knew his troubles were over temporarily, but he had fled in such haste that he had lost all traces of his path. After traveling several miles, he was hungry, thirsty and overcome with fatigue. Kneeling on the snow-covered ice, he prayed to God to direct him. Then he hurried on, he knew not where. Shortly afterward, to his great joy, he came upon his own track, which would lead him back to the wreck.

He kept going for some time. At length he heard a noise coming along the ice, like galloping horses, accompanied occasionally by a growling murmur. His strength gone, he could not make much progress. Looking back, he beheld a bear coming upon him at full speed. Soon the animal was kneeling at his feet and licking his hand. It was Nancy, and she was bleeding. She instantly turned around, then went slowly back.

He now perceived a gigantic bear standing upright, resembling a tall obelisk covered with snow. He cocked his gun and tried to run on. Nancy endeavored to stop the monster by throwing herself constantly in front of him. But the great male bear gave her a cuff with his paw to make her keep out of his way. Bruce tried several times to aim at him, but found it impossible without shooting Nancy. All he could do was stagger on. Finally, utterly exhausted, he fell flat on his face.

Instantly he found himself grasped by one of the bears. It was Nancy, trying to cover him with her own body from the attacks of the savage pursuing brute. The male struggled to reach his neck. First Bruce felt the cold nose and then the warm lips close to his throat. He called out, "Seize him!"—the words he had trained Nancy to obey in hunting. She gave the male bear such a snap that the animal desisted momentarily. Then the huge beast attacked again. Trying to reach Bruce's neck, the bear seized him by the left arm, close to the shoulder, and inflicted a deep wound. Bruce called out to his pet, who promptly seized the attacker by the throat with her teeth and paws. The beast started away, swinging her round and round like a baby, bellowing fearfully. But Nancy would not relinquish her grip. The male bear then wrapped his paws around her and threw her down.

As the two animals fought, Bruce placed the muzzle of his gun to the larger bear's ear and fired. The shot ripped away part of the beast's mouth, but his paws continued to embrace Nancy in a deadly grasp. Still she kept fast hold on his throat.

With all his waning strength, Bruce then stabbed the monster with his knife again and again. Although blood streamed through the snow as if a sluice had opened, the creature clung tenaciously to life for a few minutes. Then, with a dying gasp, he released Nancy. As soon as she got free, Bruce embraced her. Feeble and tired almost to death, they made their escape back to the old hulk.

Barricading the entrance door, Bruce fed his valiant protector, ate something himself, drank a little brandy and knelt down to return thanks to the Almighty for his strange deliverance. Having kindled a fire of coal and driftwood, he bathed and dressed his left arm, which was badly lacerated, and took a short, troubled sleep. As for Nancy, with the exertion of fighting and a hearty meal, she dozed off and on for most of the following three months, until Bruce was finally obliged to awaken her as he had done before.

It was a severe winter, much stormier than the last. By the time the sun began to show above the horizon, this Polar Crusoe had once more resolved to make a pilgrimage over the ice in search of inhabited country. Accordingly, he loaded himself and Nancy heavily with supplies. Then he left his old comfortable cabin and his mountain of ice, uncertain whether he should ever see them again.

Away they jogged together, holding a course as near as Gordon could guess to the south-southwest. At the southwest corner of the area, he unexpectedly came upon the traces of three men and a number of dogs. By following them, he arrived at a shore in a few hours.

In his attempt to overtake the men, it was necessary to leave the greater part of the supplies. He now made a muzzle for Nancy out of strong cord, for he knew she would certainly attack the dogs first and, in all probability, the men next. He set out on their track, leading his pet by a rope attached to a muzzle. She tried to get loose by pulling it off with her paws, but when he shouted at her, she stopped in bewilderment.

Fourteen hours later Bruce came to a place where the three men had evidently rested and refreshed themselves. There was a great deal of blood on the snow, and from this he concluded they were hunters and had killed game. He drank from a spring gushing out of a rock and also fed Nancy, who began scraping a spot between two rocks. He soon discovered a store of venison covered over with snow. He gathered that this spring was a hunters' rendezvous, and that to meet them he had only to remain where he was.

He soon fell asleep from fatigue and anxiety, to be awakened by Nancy struggling to get free. Hearing voices, he peeped over the rock and saw three men. Bruce drew himself up to the edge of the cliff and on his knees implored them to take him under their protection, invoking the name of the Lord. They recognized his reference to Christ, and each of them took off his fur cap and knelt on his right knee.

When Nancy appeared on the cliff, the dogs scampered off. The men were about to follow, but Bruce held up the cord to show that she was muzzled and leashed. On receiving his command, she cowered at his feet and nuzzled his hand. This astonished the men, who stared at one another. Bruce explained the situation to them as best he could in sign language, for they did not understand his tongue.

After an hour or so the men became friendly. Bruce sat down to eat with them. The meal over, they packed for departure. Taking as much food as they could transport, they yoked the dogs to sealskin bags in pairs. Bruce was afraid of a row between the dogs and Nancy. He made signs for the men to muzzle their animals, which they did. Then they started on their journey together in peace.

After proceeding for three days and three nights along the level surface of the ice, they reached the open sea and came to two canoes and a boat. Each of the men took two dogs underneath the leather of his canoe, and Bruce was deposited in the bottom of the small boat. He was forbidden to move for fear of upsetting the frail craft. Nancy obediently swam along behind the canoe, completely dominated by the commands of her master.

They crossed the sea and were met on shore by twelve young women. Bruce was conducted to their living quarters, where they were received by an old man with white hair and beard. He was the patriarch of the little colony and their priest. Bruce was instructed to kneel and receive his blessing, which he did.

The home of these simple people was strangely constructed. The outer apartments were vaulted with snow. Beside these was a long natural cavern stretching under the rocks, with many irregular side recesses. In one of these a comfortable bed was made for Bruce.

The colony consisted of thirty-one women and ten men, including the aged father—the rest of the men evidently had perished at sea or while hunting. There were seven children, two of whom were boys. Bruce was told that he was in Old Greenland among the remnant of a colony of Norwegians, a race of simple, primitive Christians whose ancestors had inhabited that bleak shore for centuries. Here, among these surroundings, Bruce lived for several months.

Nancy soon became a favorite with the entire tribe because of her fishing expertise. She accompanied them on a long expedition they made to the hulk of the *Anne Forbes,* to bring away some of the oil, spirits and iron that had been left there. On this occasion they took eight light sledges with them, drawn by thirty powerful dogs. Four men were in charge of the party, one of whom was Bruce; Nancy followed.

From the moment they returned, the bear seemed disconsolate. Her moans disturbed the whole community. One morning, after she had spent part of the night groaning as if her heart might break, she was missing. Although they searched for her far and near, she was nowhere to be found. Bruce never saw her again.

One day at the height of the summer, reports came of whaling and sealing vessels less than 150 miles to the south. Bruce decided to attempt to reach them. There were plenty of canoes, and he was given the best. He stowed supplies at his feet and then bound the sealskin around his breast. After farewells to his many friends, he set out to sea.

He continued his voyage night and day, going along the shore and landing only to sleep. He held this course until he was almost hemmed in with ice. Then he drew his canoe ashore and climbed a hill, from which he saw open sea not far away. There, to his startled eyes, were several ships, all apparently beating southward. Was he too late?

Running downhill, he leaped into the canoe and made his way to the clear water, paddling rapidly toward the fleet. Soon he realized he was being outdistanced by even the slowest craft. He reluctantly returned to shore for the night.

Next morning, after a good sleep, he again climbed the hill. To his joy, he noticed a ship far to the north, heading south in a direction that would pass his lookout post. Down the slope he ran to the canoe.

He paddled out about a mile from shore. The ship still came on. Beating up, she passed close to the canoe on one of her tacks, and Bruce's frantic shouts were heard. Heaving to, the great vessel awaited his approach. Five minutes later he was taken aboard.

He found himself on the *Briel* of Amsterdam, homeward bound to the Netherlands. From her captain he learned that he had been gone from home for seven years and one month!

Four weeks later, off Scotland, the *Briel* hailed a small fishing vessel, which took Bruce to Scotland. He went ashore in Aberdeen and eventually reached his home.

His story was received with such disbelief that he was shunned for many years as a sort of Baron Münchausen-type Scot. But as the years went by, other Scottish sailing vessels came back from the Arctic and confirmed various topographical details he had mentioned. Bruce Gordon's account was accepted by more and more people, until finally he was in good standing in the community. One of his descendants moved to America a hundred years later, and there are still many by the name of Gordon in Massachusetts.

Part Three

1800–1850

This certificate entitles you to save

50%

off the annual newsstand price of

Discover

12 issues for just $29.95.

save **50%**

☐ Payment enclosed

☐ Bill me later

In Canada, add $10 (US Funds) for postage and GST. Foreign orders add $15 (US Funds). Please allow 6–8 weeks to receive first issue. Discover's annual newsstand price is $59.88.

J9JS3

Name

Address

City   State   Zip

E-mail Address (Optional)

BUSINESS REPLY MAIL
FIRST-CLASS MAIL   PERMIT NO 150   BOONE IA

POSTAGE WILL BE PAID BY ADDRESSEE

Discover

PO BOX 37281
BOONE IA 50037-2281

1

Mutiny
on the *Somers*

"Do you fear death? Do you fear a dead man? Are you afraid to kill a man?" Thus spoke Midshipman Philip Spencer of the United States brig-of-war *Somers* on the night of November 25, 1842, to the steward, Mr. Wales. He had asked Wales to climb up into the booms so that they could converse without being overheard.

Cleverly and with great tact he talked, not revealing what was about to take place until Wales swore an oath of secrecy. Then Spencer told Wales that twenty of the crew were planning to take over the *Somers*. They would murder the commanding officer, Captain Alexander Slidell Mackenzie. Then, after choosing from the willing members of the crew who would be useful, they would kill all the others and become pirates!

Spencer stated that an inducement of the plan was the box of rare wines brought abroad when the *Somers* was at Madeira. The box also contained a large sum of money, a gift to be presented to the Commodore of the Navy on their return to the States.

When the mutineers had full charge of the vessel, Spencer proposed to sail to the Isle of Pines, a place frequented by pirates. There he had a friend who had been "in the business" before. Their plan of action was to attack only those craft they were sure to capture. After removing everything of value, they would completely destroy the vessels. Spencer and his followers would acquire all suitable women from the captured craft, use them until the pirates' interest waned, then kill them.

Spencer said that he had written out the details of this plan on the back of his cravat and would show it to Wales early the next morning. Before parting, Spencer threatened instant death should the steward reveal even one word of what had passed.

Despite the warning, next morning Wales revealed the conversation to Purser Hieskell, so that it would be communicated to the captain. Hieskell, in turn, related the story to Lieutenant Gansevoort, who immediately informed Captain Mackenzie. Although the plan seemed utterly improbable to Mackenzie, he ordered Gansevoort to keep Spencer under the closest observation without his realizing it.

After watching Spencer narrowly and inquiring among the crew about him, Gansevoort reported that the suspect had been in the wardroom examining a chart of the West Indies, and that he had questioned the assistant surgeons about the Isle of Pines, receiving the answer that it was a place much frequented by pirates. Spencer had also been observed in secret and nightly conferences with boatswain's mate F. Cromwell and seaman Elisha Small, both of whom had received money from Spencer. Bribing the wardroom steward, Spencer got him to steal brandy from the wardroom mess, brandy Spencer and several crew members drank till they were inebriated.

Although he was "servile in his intercourse" with the captain, among the crew Spencer opined that it would be "a pleasing task" to roll Mackenzie overboard off the roundhouse. At one time he drew a picture of a brig with a black flag and asked a midshipman what he thought of it. During the early part of the cruise, he had repeatedly asserted that the *Somers* might easily be taken from the Navy.

These reports together with other circumstances made Captain Mackenzie decide that something had to be done. After due consideration he ordered that all officers should lay aft on the quarterdeck except for one man stationed on the forecastle. Captain Mackenzie now approached Spencer and asked if he aspired to the command of the *Somers*. Of course, Spencer denied it.

"Did you not tell Mr. Wales, sir, that you had a project to kill the commander, the officers and a considerable portion of the crew of this vessel, and to convert her into a pirate?"

"I may have told him so, sir, but it was in joke."

"You admit, then, that you told him so?"

"Yes, sir, but in joke."

"This, sir, is joking on a forbidden subject—this joke may cost you your life! Be pleased to remove your neck handkerchief."

When nothing was found in the handkerchief, Captain Mackenzie asked Spencer, "What have you done with the paper containing an account of your project, which you told Mr. Wales was in the back of your neck handkerchief?"

"It is a paper containing my day's work, and I have destroyed it."

"It is a singular place to keep days' work in."

"It is a convenient one," Spencer replied.

"It will be necessary for me to confine you, sir." Thus speaking, Captain Mackenzie turned to Lieutenant Gansevoort with the order, "Arrest Mr. Spencer, and put him in double irons."

Gansevoort stepped forward, removed Spencer's sword and ordered him not only double ironed but handcuffed as additional security. This done, Gansevoort was directed to keep a constant watch on Spencer and to have him put to death instantly if detected speaking to any member of the crew.

Spencer's locker was searched and a small razor case was found. It contained two papers, one rolled within the other. The inner paper was covered with strange characters, which proved to be Greek. A midshipman acquainted with that language, converted the characters to English, revealing the names of the crew arranged in separate rows: the certain—the doubtful—those who were to be kept whether they would join or not—those who were to do the work of murder in the various departments, to take the wheel, to open the arms chests.

The next day the crew was inspected at ten o'clock quarters. Captain Mackenzie took his station abaft and focused his attention particularly on Cromwell, the tallest man on the brig, and Small, the shortest. That night Cromwell was brought to the quarterdeck and questioned by the captain as to a secret conversation he had had the night before with Spencer. Cromwell denied any part in it, accusing Small. When Small was brought before the captain he also made a strong denial of any guilt. But the evidence was too strong, and both men were placed in irons.

Increased vigilance was now enjoined upon all the officers. They were to be armed at all times. The captain or his first lieutenant was always on deck, and frequently both men were there. When several acts of disobedience occurred among the ship's company, punishment was inflicted to the full extent of the law, after which Captain Mackenzie addressed the crew, explaining the general nature of Spencer's plot.

Reaction to the captain's speech was varied. Many were filled with horror at the idea of the foul play they had escaped. Others were in fear of the fate that awaited them because of their connection with the conspiracy. The entire crew was under tremendous pressure. Those most seriously involved in the plot began to gather at night. Seditious words were heard, and many assumed an insolent and menacing air. Every one of the officers of the *Somers,* from the first lieutenant to the commander's clerk, proved faithful and patriotic. They were all of the opinion that the vessel was yet far from safe, that an attempt to release the prisoners was being seriously planned.

Conditions on the *Somers* were deteriorating so fast that Captain Mackenzie now instituted a thorough inspection of the crew, with the immediate arrest of the principal suspects. On November 30, 1842, he wrote a letter to all officers on board, excepting the midshipmen, asking their opinion as to what additional measures were necessary for the security of the vessel. On receipt of the letter, all the officers met in the wardroom to examine witnesses. The witnesses were duly sworn and their testimony written down; each witness signed the evidence he had given, after hearing it read to him.

Without interruption or food, the officers spent the entire day in examination and deliberation. The unanimous result of their efforts was the decision that Spencer, Cromwell and Small should be executed.

Captain Mackenzie concurred in the justice of their opinion and in the necessity of putting it into immediate effect. The petty officers were now mustered on the quarterdeck, each armed with a cutlass, pistol and cartridge box.

After all were armed, the captain spoke. "My lads! you are to look at me—to obey my orders—and to see my orders obeyed! Go forward!"

Captain Mackenzie stated that preparations for the hanging of the three principals should be made at once. All hands were called to witness the punishment.

The after guard and idlers of both watches were mustered on the quarterdeck to man the whip intended for Spencer. The forecastlemen and foretopmen made ready for Cromwell, to whose influence they had been chiefly exposed. And the main-topmen of both watches were at the whip for Small, who for a month or more had been captain of the maintop. The officers and petty officers were stationed about the decks, with orders to cut down whoever should let go the whip with even one hand or fail to haul on it when so ordered. The ensign and pennant were bent on and ready for hoisting.

Captain Mackenzie now put on his full uniform and prepared to carry out the most painful duty ever asked of an American commander: to tell three of his own men of their final fate. Going up to Spencer, he said: "When you were about to take my life, and to dishonor me as an officer while in the execution of my rightful duty, without cause or offense to you, on speculation, it was your intention to remove me suddenly from the world, in the darkness of the night, in my sleep, without a moment to utter one whisper of affection to my wife and children—one prayer for their welfare. Your life is now forfeited to your country; and the necessities of the case, growing out of your corruption of the crew, compel me to take it. I will not, however, imitate your intended example as to the manner of claiming the sacrifice. If there yet remains to you one feeling true to nature, it shall be gratified. If you have any word to send to your parents, it shall be recorded and faithfully delivered. Ten minutes shall be granted you for this purpose."

Spencer was overcome and sank to his knees, sobbing, until Captain Mackenzie reminded him of his duty as an officer to die with decorum. The captain then spoke to Cromwell and Small. The former protested that he was innocent, and Spencer supported his claim. But Lieutenant Gansevoort and the petty officers agreed that Cromwell was guilty beyond the shadow of a doubt.

Captain Mackenzie returned again to Spencer and asked if he had any messages for his family. Spencer replied: "Tell them that I die wishing them every blessing and happiness. I deserve death for this and many other crimes. There are few crimes that I have not committed. I feel sincerely penitent, and my only fear of death is that my repentance may be too late. I have wronged many persons, but chiefly my parents. This will kill my poor mother! I do not know what would have become of me had I succeeded. I fear this may injure my father.* I will tell you frankly what I intended to do, had I got home—I should have attempted to escape. I had the same project on board the *John Adams* and *Potomac*. It seemed to be a mania with me."

Spencer questioned whether the law would justify the commander taking life under such circumstances. Captain Mackenzie assured him that it would; that he had consulted all his brother officers, his messmates included, except the

---

* Spencer was the son of the Honorable John C. Spencer, Secretary of War under President Tyler, who held that position at the time of his son's disgrace.

boys, and their opinion was just, and that he deserved death.

Spencer now asked for a Bible and a prayer book. After a short time he stated that he begged forgiveness for what he had planned against the captain, at which Captain Mackenzie shook hands with Spencer. The prisoners were then escorted to the gangway. At the break of the quarterdeck was a narrow passage between the trunk and the pump-well. Spencer and Cromwell met on either side. Cromwell was told to stop in order to allow Spencer to pass first. Spencer asked to talk with Mr. Wales, who then came forward.

"Mr. Wales," said Spencer, "I earnestly hope you will forgive me for tampering with your fidelity."

Wales, almost overcome with emotion, replied, "I do forgive you from the bottom of my heart, and I hope that God will forgive you also."

Spencer now walked on, meeting Small at the gangway. Spencer extended his hand and asked forgiveness, but Small drew back with horror.

"No, by God! I can't forgive you!"

Spencer asked again, and after a brief pause Small, at the urging of Captain Mackenzie, stated in a subdued voice that he forgave Spencer, and the two men shook hands.

Small was placed on the hammocks forward of the gangway, with his face inboard. Spencer was similarly placed abaft the gangway, with Cromwell on the other side of him.

Spencer asked the captain what was to be the signal for execution. Mackenzie answered that he wished to hoist the colors at the moment of execution, so it was his plan to beat to call as for hoisting the colors, then roll off, and at the third roll fire a gun. Spencer asked to be allowed to give the word to fire the gun, and his request was granted. He then begged that no interval might elapse between giving the word and firing the gun.

Now Small asked to address the crew. "Shipmates and top-mates! Take warning by my example. I never was a pirate. I never killed a man. It's for saying I would do it that I am about to depart this life. See what a word will do!" He turned to Spencer. "I am now ready to die, Mr. Spencer. Are you?"

Cromwell's last words were, "Tell my wife I die an innocent man. Tell Lieutenant Morris I die an innocent man."

All was ready. But then Spencer, who was to give the signal, stated that he could not give it and asked Captain Mackenzie to do so.

The signal was given, and the execution by hanging was carried out. Thus it was that three Navy men were swung out into eternity from the yardarm of the brig *Somers*.

The crew was ordered aft at once. All hands were called to "cheer the ship," as the saying went more than a century ago. Captain Mackenzie himself gave the order: "Stand by to give three hearty cheers for the flag of our country!" Never were three heartier cheers given.

On the following Sunday the captain addressed the crew, telling them that as they had shown they could give cheers for their country, they should now cheer their God in song. The colors were then hoisted and above the American ensign, the only banner to which it may give place: the banner of the cross. Then every member of the ship's company, officers and crew, joined in singing the one-hundredth psalm.

When the *Somers* eventually reached home, the mutiny and execution were investigated by a court of inquiry made up of Commodores Stewart, Jones and Dallas. Captain Mackenzie's action was fully approved. Mackenzie himself requested that a court-martial be held. Commodore John Downes was president. The trial, which lasted forty days, resulted in Mackenzie's acquittal.

Thus the insidious action of Philip Spencer in the year 1842 aboard the brig-of-war *Somers* is recorded for all generations as the first regularly organized mutiny in the annals of the naval history of the United States of America.

2

The Murdered Minister

One pleasant day in October 1827 the Reverend Mr. Charles Sharply rode into Alfred, Maine, and held services in the meetinghouse there. After the sermon he announced that he was going to Waterboro to preach, and that on his circuit he had collected $270 to help build a church in that village. Would not his hearers add to that sum? They would and did, and that evening the parson rode away with over $300 in his saddlebags. He never appeared in Waterboro or any other village or settlement again.

Various reasons were suggested by the country people, many of whom believed that possession of the money had made him forget his sacred calling and leave the State of Maine with his spoils.

On the morning after Reverend Sharply's disappearance, the church deacon, Nathaniel Dickerman, appeared in the town of Alfred riding on a horse that some believed was the minister's. The tavern hostler, however, affirmed that the minister's horse had a white star on his forehead and breast, whereas the horse the deacon was riding was all black.

Deacon Dickerman explained that he had found the horse grazing in his yard at daybreak, and that he would give it to anyone who could prove it to be his property. Since nobody appeared to demand it, he kept the animal. People soon forgot that it was not his. The deacon extended his business shortly after this and prospered. With wealth, he became sullen and averse to company.

One day a rumor went around that a belated traveler had seen a misty apparition under "the owl tree" at a turn in the road where owls were hooting, and that it took on a strange likeness to the missing clergyman. Deacon Dickerman paled when he heard the story, but he shook his head and muttered about the folly of listening to stupid nonsense.

The years went by, a decade since the minister had vanished. During that time the boys of the town had avoided the owl tree after dark. Then one afternoon a clergyman of the neighborhood was hastily summoned to see Deacon Dickerman, who was said to be suffering from overwork. He found the deacon in his house alone, pacing the floor, his clothing disarrayed, his cheeks strangely flushed. He asked the clergyman to listen to a statement he wished to make.

"My time in this world is almost ended," said Nathaniel Dickerman, "nor would I live longer if I could. I am haunted day and night, and there is no peace, no rest for me on earth. They say that Sharply's spirit has appeared at the owl tree. Well, his body lies there. They accused me of taking his horse. It is true. A little black dye on his head and breast was all that was needed to deceive them. Pray for me, for I fear my soul is lost. I killed Sharply."

The clergyman recoiled.

"I killed him," the wretched Dickerman went on, "for the money that he had. The devil prospered me with it. In my will I leave two thousand dollars to his widow and five thousand dollars to the church he was collecting for. Will there be mercy for me? I dare not think it. Go and pray for me."

The clergyman hastened to leave but was hardly outside the door when the report of a pistol brought him back. Dickerman lay dead on the floor. Sharply's skeleton was found and removed from the shade of the owl tree, and as far as is known the area around the tree was never haunted afterward.

3

Drowned at Sea

At the height of a great storm a frantic woman, faced with death and almost out of her mind from worry, clung to her baby son on the deck of a stranded bark. Wave after wave smashed into the vessel, and she realized that she could not keep up the unequal fight much longer.

The woman in mortal terror was Margaret Fuller, recognized today as one of the most brilliant and scholarly American women of the nineteenth century. In the field of female intelligence, she dominated her century as Anne Hutchinson did hers. Both were either bitterly condemned or extravagantly praised.

Margaret Fuller once stated, "If all the wicked people submitted to be drowned, the world would be a desert." Her own fate during a shipwreck was indeed a weird contrast to her remarks.

Margaret Fuller, who became Marchesa Ossoli, was an American writer born May 23, 1810, in Cambridge, Massachusetts. Early in Margaret's life her father, Timothy Fuller, recognized her brilliance and trained her to be a "youthful prodigy."

It is said that Margaret danced her way through Harvard College with members of the class of 1829. This class has been

made too famous by the wit and poetry of Oliver Wendell
Holmes not to be considered among the most eminent that
ever left Harvard. The memory of one lady has preserved for us
a picture of the girl Margaret as she appeared at a ball when
she was sixteen. "She had a very plain face, half-shut eyes,
and hair curled all over her head; she was dressed in a badly-
cut, low-neck pink silk with white muslin over it; and she
danced quadrilles very awkwardly, being withal so near-
sighted that she could hardly see her partner."

Margaret Fuller became one of the backers of Brook Farm in
West Roxbury, and frequently appeared at this famous headquarters of transcendentalism. Unfortunately, about this time
she incurred the everlasting resentment of Nathaniel Hawthorne. Gentle as the great writer was by birth and upbringing,
he was outstandingly harsh and bitter in his comments on
Brook Farm and on the woman he called Zenobia, in reality
Margaret Fuller. Elsewhere in his writings he indicated that
the Marchesa was definitely not one of his particular favorites:
"Margaret Fuller had a strong and coarse nature which she
had done her utmost to refine, with infinite pains; but, of
course, it could be only superficially changed. . . . Margaret
has not left in the hearts and minds of those who knew her any
deep witness of her integrity and purity. She was a great hum-
bug."

Although Margaret was known as the high priestess of the
transcendental movement, early in its operation she detected
several of its outstanding flaws.

Then, when her father died, Miss Fuller taught languages
in the Alcott School. In 1837 she became a "principal teacher"
in the Green Street School, Providence, Rhode Island, to fulfill
her responsibilities for her brothers' and sisters' education.

In December 1844 Horace Greeley brought her to New York
to put the literary criticism of the *Tribune* on a higher plane
than any other American newspaper. He also gave her an
opportunity to discuss in a broad and stimulating way all
philanthropic questions.

While on the *Tribune* Margaret Fuller put aside money for a journey to Europe, a trip that had been her lifelong dream. At last, on the first of August 1846, she sailed away.

Soon after Miss Fuller's arrival in Rome, early in 1847, she went one day to hear vespers at St. Peter's. Becoming separated from her friends after the service, she was observed in the church by a young man of gentlemanly address, who offered his services as a guide.

Not seeing her friends anywhere, she let the young Marchese Ossoli accompany her home. They met once or twice again before she left Rome for the summer. The following season Miss Fuller had an apartment in Rome. She often received among her guests this young patriot who had her sympathy and with whose labors in behalf of his native city she was so thoroughly in agreement.

When the Marchese proposed, Margaret refused to marry him, insisting that he should choose a younger woman for his wife. At length he convinced her of his sincere love and affection, and she married him in December 1847.

She served in hospitals while Ossoli was in the army outside the city. In September 1848 their child, Angelo, was born. The happy family went to Florence.

On May 17, 1850, together with her husband, her son Angelo and a maid, Margaret boarded the bark *Elizabeth* at Leghorn, bound for the United States. She brought with her a precious manuscript of the struggle for Italian liberty in which she and her husband had been involved.

For the twenty-three persons aboard the *Elizabeth* it was a voyage of terror almost from the beginning. Two days after the ship sailed, the captain came down with smallpox and was confined to his bunk. He never recovered, dying a few days later. The inexperienced mate took charge of the bark, and the *Elizabeth* stopped at Gibraltar before resuming her voyage.

A short time later Angelo became ill with smallpox, but Margaret was able to nurse him back to health.

By July 17 the *Elizabeth* was near New York. Late that

afternoon a gale began and the unhappy mate soon admitted that he had lost his bearings. Although Jeannette Edward Rattray * relates that the mate was reasonably certain the *Elizabeth* was off the New Jersey coast, at four o'clock in the morning of July 17 the bark was wrecked on a sandbar off Fire Island, near Point O'Woods, New York.

The bark stayed afloat for some time, but the waves were so high that no one dared launch a lifeboat. A few of the passengers and several crew members managed to reach shore on planks. Margaret Fuller, holding her child in her arms, sat on the deck at the foot of the mainmast. Clad only in her nightgown and shawl, with the wind whipping her long hair, she refused to leave the ship. The steward, noting that the mainmast was about to fall, seized the child and jumped overboard. Both were drowned, as were Margaret's husband and their maid when waves washed them out of the rigging. Margaret went down with the bark alone. Ten others were lost in the sea, while twelve saved their own lives.

A bronze tablet was erected on Fire Island near Point O'Woods in memory of Margaret Fuller, but later it too was lost because of the encroachment of the sea.

Marchesa Ossoli and her husband had been fearful as they embarked on the fated ship that was to take them to America. Ossoli had been cautioned by a fortune-teller when he was a boy to beware of the sea, and his wife had long cherished a superstition that the year 1850 would be a marked epoch in her life. In writing to a friend about her fear, Margaret said, "I pray that if we are lost it may be brief anguish, and Ossoli, the babe, and I go together."

The bodies of the parents were never recovered, but that of little Angelo was discovered and buried in a seaman's chest among the sandhills. The child's remains were later disinterred and brought to Mount Auburn Cemetery in Cambridge by relatives who never saw the baby in life.

* Author of *Ship Ashore*.

The letters that passed between the young nobleman and the wife he adored are still extant, having been found with her baby. They are the only things of Margaret Fuller's saved from the fatal wreck in which she and her two loved ones were drowned. Her manuscript of the Italian struggle was lost forever.

So at Mount Auburn, in the same cemetery where Longfellow, Agassiz, Booth, Winslow Homer, Julia Ward Howe and a host of others are buried, the unfortunate waif lies in a neglected area of the great burial ground.

4

Miraculous Escape from the *Adelaide*

A shipwreck with a strange aftermath quite similar to the *Cod Seeker* * occurred at Barnegat, New Jersey, on September 10, 1846. Bound out of Manahawkin, the sloop *Adelaide* was attempting to reach Barnegat Inlet before a severe gale hit the coast. Crashing into the bar, the *Adelaide* capsized. Captain James Lamson and his entire crew drowned almost instantly.

The vessel, still bottom up, pounded through the breakers and finally went ashore some distance from Barnegat Light. Lighthouse keeper John Allen, former keeper Garret H. Herring and young Charles Collins watched the wreck push in toward the beach. Around dusk, just before the tide would turn and come in, it appeared that by careful attention to safety they could probably get on the bottom of the craft and inspect it. Realizing that the captain and crew had perished, they were eager to see what could be salvaged, for the *Adelaide*'s crew were all natives of Barnegat. At almost dead low water Herring and Collins started to go down the beach; Allen had to stay behind to trim the wicks and light the lamps for the night.

After reaching the *Adelaide*, which apparently was burying

* See my *Tales of Terror and Tragedy*, pp. 200ff.

herself in the sand, they waited for a particularly huge wave to recede. Then they jumped nimbly aboard.

As the two men walked along the slippery hull, the surf roared in and out, sand and gravel scraped against the sides and the vessel rocked back and forth. But suddenly there came a different sound—a dull pounding. At first they paid no attention. Then the noise grew louder and more insistent. Could it be that someone was still inside the hull, imprisoned by the water and sand, and was thumping on the bottom to attract attention?

Just then Keeper Allen, high in the tower, turned on Barnegat Light. The two figures atop the wreck watched as the steady beam shone through the gathering darkness.

"There's someone or something still alive in there," shouted Herring above the roar of the surf. "You and I have got to break through and reach them. We'll have our hands full, what with the tide coming in and darkness coming on. You are a lot younger than I am, so you start running for the lighthouse. Get the two axes in the storeroom and a lantern, and come back as soon as you can."

Young Charlie Collins raced along the bottom of the vessel, leaped high on the sand and broke out in a fast dash for the lighthouse. Breathlessly he told his story, got the needed articles and returned to the wreck. But even the twenty minutes he had taken made it just a little harder to climb aboard the hull of the *Adelaide*, for the gathering storm was now sweeping in rapidly.

"Good work, boy," said Herring. "I've located the tapping. It's right here below me, where the cabin is. We have a chance, if we're quick."

The two fell to work with the axes by the light of the lantern. Within twenty minutes, between surges from the sea, they had chopped a hole in the bottom of the ship. Herring grabbed the lantern and thrust it inside.

"Wait just a little longer," he shouted down into the darkness.

The answer he received astounded him. "I will," said a girl's voice!

They chopped all the faster, for with the incoming tide it did not seem possible that the girl, whom they judged to be a teenager, could live under such conditions much longer.

Just then a terrific wave hit the *Adelaide,* rushing through, over and under the craft. A great spurt of water shot out of the small hole the men had made in the bottom.

"Hold on. We'll get you out in a minute!" cried Herring. He knew that if they did not hurry, the cabin would soon become a tomb.

Again and again the axes smashed into the vessel. Slowly but surely the opening widened to a point where the girl could almost clamber out.

At the moment she was about to attempt her escape, a towering wave began to build up just off the bow of the overturned vessel.

"Give me both hands," Herring shouted. A moment later two wet, bleeding arms were thrust out as far as the broken section of the hull would allow. Collins had cut a piece of line from the wreck. As Herring held the girl's hands, Collins began to secure each of her wrists.

Just then the billow struck. Smashing toward shore with terrific force, it actually jarred the *Adelaide* from her deeply imbedded position in the sand, overwhelming the craft, filling the tiny cabin and burying the men with foam. Herring clung desperately to the girl. A moment later the wave began to recede.

Now was their chance. Collins secured her wrists so that another wave would not smash her around inside the cabin.

"We'll have you out in just a little while," Herring reassured her. "We've got you tied so that whenever there is a bad wave you won't drown. For now, clamber back in the cabin away from the hole, and we'll chop away a little more of the bulkhead. Then I think you'll be able to climb out."

By the light of the lantern the men desperately crashed their axes against the hull, widening the opening. Just as another towering breaker was about to smash into the wreck, they pulled the bleeding, frightened survivor from her prison.

The three huddled there, clinging to each other and the craft as the wave inundated the hulk. After it subsided, the men guided the girl to the shore side of the wreck, helping her down through the swirling water. Ten minutes later they were at the lighthouse, where the victim began to recover from the stark terror of her experience.

She was the daughter of Captain James Lamson, a widower who had taken her along on the voyage. The *Adelaide* had turned over and was driven onto the bar after the girl's father sent her below for safety. She did not know what had happened to the others because the capsizing had enclosed her in the fearsome darkness of the upside-down cabin. Evidently the air had been compressed into a corner and she had clung there, holding on to the bunk.

As the *Adelaide* was pushed shoreward by the waves, time and again the bunk was submerged in water and Miss Lamson * had to hold her breath. The compressed air, which she could breathe every time the boat went back to an even keel, kept her alive. But the hole that was chopped in the *Adelaide* let out the compressed air, and the surf rushed through whenever a wave hit the craft. It was a miracle she was still alive.

After putting her to bed and getting word to her relatives, the keeper's wife made a hot supper. The following week a fisherman named Worden, who hailed from Forked River and was a friend of the Lamsons, proposed to Miss Lamson. The offer was eventually accepted and they were married.

The couple's little girl, Katherine, arrived two years later. She was frequently taken by her mother to the scene of her grandfather's death and her mother's miraculous escape. Katy grew up on the seashore and fell in love with a Sandy Hook pilot named Carr. They were married sometime after the Civil War. Together they often visited Barnegat Light on the anniversary of the wreck.

* Her first name has not come down to us.

5

Tom Dunn's Dance

Vermont's Rag Rock, in which the famous Indian Wabanowi began his long sleep in 1767, was the home of demons and sprites as late as the nineteenth century. Indian scout Thomas Dunn was aware of this, and ordinarily he would take a long maneuver to avoid contact with the creatures of the spirit world. However, one night when he had occupied himself with what historian C. M. Skinner called "keeping his spirits up by pouring spirits down," and had kissed his pretty partner at the husking bee twenty times, he decided to take a chance and cut right across the hill so famous for the demons and sprites he usually feared.

Approaching the top of the hill, he observed a glow through the trees, and soon heard a fiddle "going like mad." With determination he forced his way through the thickets to discover who was holding a picnic in the moonshine of the evening. When he listened carefully, he distinctly heard the rustle of feet.

Arriving at the edge of the glade, he saw a richly dressed and merry company surrounded by a dozen torches. Each person was dancing with extremely vivacious spirit.

Tom, who dearly loved to participate in a jig or a reel, could

not possibly ignore this chance. When he entered the ring
where the people were enjoying themselves, he was greeted
with a tremendous shout. While sitting on a hummock of
moss, he noticed a maiden fair who lacked a partner. She had
snapping black eyes, rosy cheeks and lips apparently inviting.
The skirts she wore were just a speck higher than the custom
of the period, and her ankles were indeed acceptable to all who
saw them.

Catching her by the waist, Tom started whirling with her
into the middle of the gayest, most extraordinary dance in
which he had ever participated. He felt himself soaring into
the sky. As he glanced around the ring, he realized that all the
other dancers had quit their activity to sit on the edge of the
ring and watch him. Then the music of the violin, starting
with an especially catchy note, made him kick his heels in the
air, cracking them before he came down in an ecstasy that
combined both motion and existence itself.

Round after round of applause greeted him. He and the
pretty girl decided to separate half a dozen feet and dance each
other down. After a strenuous twenty minutes, Tom noticed
uneasily that the early freshness was vanishing from the girl's
features. Her eyes, becoming harder and deeper, began to turn
from black to light green. Her teeth began to push out of her
mouth, turning sharp and yellow, and her lips curved in an
evil grin. He realized with a shudder that he was in the company of the demon group of the hill!

He knew that if he could not keep dancing until dawn, or
the setting of the moon, he was doomed. He began to fling off
his clothing—first his coat, then his hat, finally his vest and
tie. By this time the moon was beginning to set. In two hours
he would be free.

All seemed well until a cramp caught him in the calf and he
knew he could not last. With a cry of desperation, he cried,
"God save me!" and fell over on his back.

That cry did save him, for no witch or spirit, it is said, can
endure to even hear the name of God. All Tom saw was a brief

vision of scurrying forms going in every direction, hissing, growling and uttering curses.

Suddenly a hideous shape was hanging right over him in a terribly threatening fashion. He had the feeling that his time had come, that he was going to die. The strong smell of sulphur overcame him, and then he knew no more.

Hours later he awakened in the brilliant sunshine of a new day. Wondering if the strenuous carousal of the night before had been only the imaginings of a mind befogged by alcohol, he glanced around the clearing. Everywhere was evidence of high activity. Beside him lay his jacknife. Tom picked it up and was shocked when he looked at the handle: etched in fire were two portraits of the witch with whom he had begun his dance in happiness and ended it in terror. One portrait showed her in the full blossom of youth, the other as she appeared in her final decrepitude, hanging over him in that last frightening moment.

Tom Dunn soon suffered a high fever. When it ended he decided what he should do, and he did it with a vengeance. Calling on a desirable woman of his own age, he courted her briefly and then proposed. Soon after that he began to attend church regularly, married the girl who was not exactly of his dreams, forsook all entertainments, drank tea and became a steady workman.

For the remainder of his many years he enjoyed peace of mind, eventually dying a deacon of his church. In recognition of his good character, on his gravestone was carved a cherub similar to those on the organ loft of the Old North Church in Boston. But it was different in one striking way. The cherub on Tom Dunn's stone, for some mysterious reason, suffered a sculptured toothache.

A model of the seven-masted *Thomas W. Lawson.* The schooner's namesake was a financial genius with outside interests ranging from yacht racing to Republican politics to a $30,000 pink carnation named for his wife.

Hermit Mason Walton's articles and book put him in a class with Henry David Thoreau and John Burroughs. The malaise of city life led Walton to eighteen years of "hermiting" that brought him recognition as one of the world's oustanding naturalists.

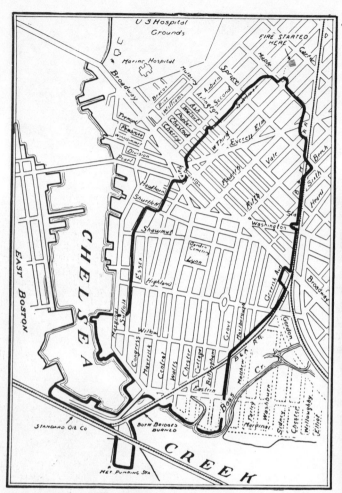

The map of Chelsea, Massachusetts, shows the section
ravaged by fire on Palm Sunday, 1908. Refugees carting
valuables—including a terrified cat in a parrot cage—
clogged the street in search of safety.

More than two thousand Electric Company employees and family members boarded the steamer *Eastland* on the morning of July 24, 1915, eagerly anticipating their fifth annual excursion trip and picnic. The "cranky ship" listed from side to side at its Chicago pier, then suddenly rolled over and sank on the bottom of the river like a massive whale. Nearby crafts raced to the scene, and people on shore quickly threw all available floatable objects into the water. No crew members were lost in the disaster, but for 835 passengers this was their last excursion. *(Courtesy Chicago Historical Society)*

LT. GEN. SIR WM. PEPPERRELL, Bart.
The Victor of Louisbourg A.D. 1745.

The siege of Louisbourg in 1745 seemed akin to a vacation tour. But the hastily assembled army of American country squires, merchants, farmers and fishermen, led by prosperous trader William Pepperrell, captured the French stronghold with surprising ease.

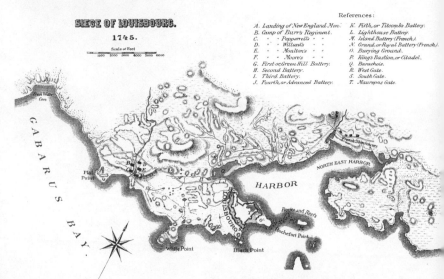

SIEGE OF LOUISBOURG.

1745.

Scale of Feet
1000 2000 3000 4000 5000 6000

References:

A. *Landing of New England Men.*
B. *Camp of Burr's Regiment.*
C.   " " *Pepperrell's* " "
D.   " " *Willard's* " "
E.   " " *Moulton's* " "
F.   " " *Moore's* " "
G. *First or Green Hill Battery.*
H. *Second Battery.*
I. *Third Battery.*
J. *Fourth, or Advanced Battery.*

K. *Fifth, or Titcomb's Battery.*
L. *Lighthouse Battery.*
M. *Island Battery (French).*
N. *Grand, or Royal Battery (French).*
O. *Burying Ground.*
P. *King's Bastion, or Citadel.*
Q. *Barrachois.*
R. *West Gate.*
S. *South Gate.*
T. *Maurepas Gate.*

All 191 passengers and crew members aboard the *Portland* were lost in a November gale off Cape Cod. Captain Hollis H. Blanchard tried to no avail to summon help from the Race Point LIfe Saving Station. *(Photo of Blanchard courtesy Al Snow of Chatham)*

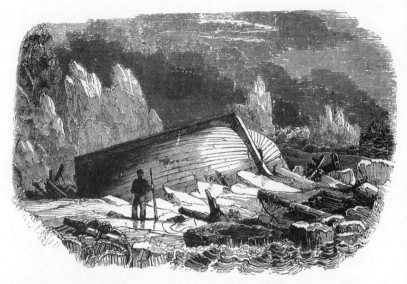

When the whaling ship *Anne Forbes* was crushed by icebergs in the great polar ocean, Seaman Bruce Gordon was thrown onto a field of ice—the only survivor. For the next seven years he lived aboard the resurfaced vessel, alone except for the companionship of a faithful polar bear he named Nancy. After his rescue, Gordon's incredible tale was disbelieved for many years until other sailors confirmed various details.

As a child Mary Sawyer Tyler rescued a newborn lamb forsaken by its mother—and thus went on to fame in John Roulstone's poem of Mary and her little lamb. "If I had known that...my little pet would give me such notoriety," said Mrs. Tyler, "I do not know that I should have carried out the plan I did."

Midshipman Philip Spencer of the brig-of-war *Somers* attempted the first organized mutiny in U.S. naval history. the plot was revealed to the captain, who searched the brig and obtained evidence. Spencer and his two principal cohorts, Elisha Small and F. Cromwell, were whipped and then hanged from the yardarm.

Part Four

1850–1900

1

The Inherited Curse

When Sir Anthony Brown, Knight of the Garter, centuries ago took possession of Battle Abbey and Caldray in the British Isles, awarded to him by Henry VIII for services rendered, the monks are said to have placed a curse upon him and his descendants for evicting them, vowing that fire and flood would always follow his family.

A direct descendant of Sir Anthony, Mrs. S. Fahs Smith of York, Pennsylvania, collected information that indicates the curse—if curse it was—actually did influence the lives of many of Sir Anthony's descendants. The husband of Mrs. Smith's aunt, Laura, was drowned about 1870 when getting off a ship at Charleston, South Carolina. Aunt Laura died from taking poison by mistake in 1872. Two of Charles Mitchell's nieces drowned while passengers on the S.S. *Champion,* which collided with another craft en route to Charleston, around 1878. In 1900 Charles Mitchell's nephew, Mr. Bramwell of Flushing, New York, was sitting on the shore at a resort in New Jersey. After handing his watch to his fiancée, he went into the water and was attacked and eaten by a shark. Burwell Smith's yacht was lost off Cuba in 1947. This chapter concerns the terrible affair of the steamer *Arctic,* on which Mrs. Smith's father, Charles Mitchell, sailed in the year 1854.

Charles Mitchell had taken his sister Caroline to London, and they were planning to return aboard the *Arctic*. On the night before they were to sail, Caroline had a terrifying nightmare. She decided it was a warning not to sail on the *Arctic;* Charles Mitchell agreed to cancel her passage. However, because he was anxious to see his family, he sailed without her. That decision almost cost him his life.

The *Arctic* was launched on January 28, 1850, at William H. Brown's East River yard. She was the third of four wooden-hull, paddle-wheel steamships of the New York and Liverpool United States Mail Steamship Company, usually referred to as the Collins Line. She was capable of breaking the transatlantic record of the period, and did so on her February 1852 crossing. On the average, all the Collins liners were much faster than the Cunarders.

The 284-foot *Arctic* was such a beautiful ship that she soon became the talk of two continents. *Harper's* magazine for June 1852 stated, "Never did there float upon the ocean a more magnificent palace." John S. Abbott, writer of the article, described the main cabin, with its carcel * lamps, highly polished satinwood and rosewood, beautiful mirrors, "stained glass, silver plate, costly carpets, marble center tables, luxurious sofas and arm chairs," plus a "profusion of rich gilding giving an air of almost Oriental magnificence to a room 100 feet in length and 25 in breadth."

It was indeed a remarkable ship. Congressman Barry of Mississippi later said: "If they had spent in lifeboats for that vessel the money they spent in gingerbread ornaments and decorations, there might have been hundreds of valuable lives saved."

The *Arctic* left Liverpool on her ill-fated voyage for New York September 20, 1854, with more than 250 passengers and a crew of 140. Among the passengers were many of wealth and distinction. The wife, son and daughter of Mr. Collins,

---

* A mechanical lamp named for its inventor, B. G. Carcel, in which the oil is pumped to the wick by clockwork.

owner of the line, were aboard, and the Duc de Gramont was one of the distinguished names on the passenger list. Captain James C. Luce, commander of the ship, had with him his crippled eight-year-old son who, it was hoped, would benefit from the sea voyage.

New Englanders aboard included a Bostonian, Mr. A. Stone, and his family. Frederick W. Gale from Worcester, Massachusetts, together with his wife, child and servant had been traveling in Italy and had lived in Florence for some weeks. A young married couple named Lang hailed from Massachusetts. Mrs. John Childe and her daughter were from Springfield. Benjamin W. Copes, his wife and child were said to have been aboard, as well as "R. S. Williams & Lady" of Salem. Mrs. Howland and her son, relatives of Dr. Williams of Boston, also made the fatal trip, together with M. M. Day, his wife and daughter of Salem.

A week passed at sea without bad weather. The Collins liner reached the Grand Banks, and all aboard were expecting to arrive at New York three days later, on September 30. September 27 was calm and hazy. Occasional low-lying fog moved into the area. Although a sailor was often stationed in the forecastle head to blow on a horn at intervals, Captain Luce did not consider it foggy enough for this precaution.

At noon the captain took his observations for latitude. All who had entered the pool for guessing the day's run were anxiously awaiting announcement of the ship's position, but Luce never finished making his calculations. Suddenly the lookout in the bow gave a shout of alarm, and almost at once the officer of the deck told the man at the wheel to change the course "hard to starboard."

"I rushed on deck," said the captain later, "and just got out when I felt a crash forward and at the same moment saw a strange steamer under the starboard bow. In another moment she struck against the guards of the *Arctic* and passed astern of us. The bows of the strange ship appeared to be cut off literally for about ten feet. Seeing that in all probability she must sink in a few minutes, after taking a hasty glance at our own ship and believing that we were comparatively uninjured, my first impulse was to try to save the lives of those on board the stranger."

Immediately Captain Luce ordered two of the *Arctic*'s lifeboats lowered. His chief officer, Robert J. Gourlay, and six seamen rowed over to the vessel to see if help was needed. Later it was found that the craft with which the *Arctic* had collided was the 200-ton French steamer *Vesta,* on the way back to France from the island of Miquelon with 197 fishermen and sailors aboard. She suffered appalling damage but was able to stay afloat.

Just when the lifeboats were lowered, Captain Luce heard that the *Arctic* herself was in serious trouble. The collision had not been felt at all on the *Arctic.* No one in the engine room realized what had happened when they received the sign for "full astern." A few minutes later, however, Chief Engineer J. W. Rogers saw an ominous flow of black bilge water beginning to swirl around the engine bed plates. He opened the bilge injector at once, allowing the giant jet condensers of the main engine to suck water from the bilge. But the flow continued to gain, and soon Mr. Rogers realized that the *Arctic* was doomed.

In addition to water pouring into the engine room, it was also coming into the ship through several holes in the bow, the largest of which was more than five feet long and eighteen inches wide. No less than a thousand gallons a second were swirling into the hull.

Captain Luce ordered a sail passed over the bow to cover the leaks, but a large part of the *Arctic*'s stem and her broken iron anchor prevented a snug fit. Carpenter George Baily volunteered to go over the side in a boatswain's chair to attempt stuffing pillows and mattresses into the holes. By the time they began to lower him, the *Arctic* was so far down by the head that the operation was abandoned as impossible.

Inside the hull Boatswain Thomas Wilde was also desperately attempting to plug the leak. When the water reached the cargo, he realized he could do nothing more.

Captain Luce was now faced with a terrible decision. Should he continue his attempt to stop the leaks, or put all efforts toward a mad dash for the nearest land, fifty miles away at Cape Race, Newfoundland? He finally decided on the latter alternative. By this time Gourlay's lifeboat had disappeared in the fog, and the steamer *Vesta* had also vanished. Luce believed she had already gone down.

Now occurred one of the terrifying incidents of the disaster. The *Arctic* had just begun her desperate dash for shore when a horrifying scream pierced the air. Coming out of the fog, directly in the *Arctic*'s path, was a lifeboat that had been launched by the *Vesta*. Before anyone could do anything, the boat was caught under the *Arctic*'s paddle wheel and eleven men were ground to pieces. Only one of the twelve occupants was saved: François Gajoick, a French-Canadian fisherman. He was hauled aboard, then the *Arctic* continued through the icy seas in a desperate gamble to reach land.

Meanwhile, in the *Arctic*'s hold, the seawater was rising higher and higher. When it reached the ash pits and the bottom grates, the lower fires were extinguished one by one and the firemen were forced to flee topside to save their lives. The paddle wheels continued to turn rapidly. The upper fires soon went out as well. This was the beginning of the end, for the paddles began to slow down. Then, with a last indecisive churning, they stopped.

Only an hour had passed since the two craft had come together. Captain Luce's gamble had failed, but he had developed other plans for saving the women and children in the five remaining lifeboats. When the paddles stopped, however, uncontrolled panic broke out. A group of men leaped into the stern boat and cut her loose at once. What happened on the next lifeboat was written by a passenger, Mr. F. DeMaeyer:

"The boat was then ordered to be lowered, but before letting it down to the water, the passengers were placed in it to secure it against seizure of the ship's crew. Twenty-five passengers, of whom eighteen were ladies, and among them Mrs. Collins, were placed in it, when one rope at the stern end of the boat gave way, hanging it by the bows and precipitating all into the ocean except two men (one of them was Thomas Stinson, officer's steward) and Mrs. Craig, who clung to the boat. The lady was again taken on board the ship, and the boat with the two men in it was immediately put afloat. As soon as it was on the water a rush was made for it, passengers and crew together jumping from the ship, some falling in the water and others into the boat."

All but one of the remaining lifeboats were taken over by mobs of men and cut adrift. In the last boat the chief engineer placed a group of fifteen and rowed it out to a position near the *Arctic*.

Captain Luce now decided to make a raft on which many of the survivors could find refuge, and he gave all the women passengers life preservers. Along with examples of cowardice among the men, there were many instances of courage and even heroism. A young apprentice engineer, Stewart Holland of Washington, had been given the task of firing the signal gun at minute intervals. This he did continuously until the ship sank beneath him. His last act was the final firing of the gun as he was engulfed by the sea.

When the raft was almost ready, an alarm went around the ship that the *Arctic* was about to go under. This created a terrifying rush for the raft. Captain Luce almost tore the shirt off Fireman Patrick Tobin's back, attempting to restrain him.

"It was every man for himself," said Tobin later. "Life was as sweet to us as life to others."

At 4:45 that afternoon the stern dipped under the water, the bow rose in the air and the ship began her fateful plunge stern first. Passenger George Burns remembered "one fearful shriek . . . but the most terrible noise of all, which drowned other sounds, was the ship's own death moans as air trapped below made its final escape through the smokestack with an all but human-sounding wail, awful to hear."

Captain Luce, holding his little boy, went down with the ship but floated up to the surface. After struggling with the child in his arms, he was sucked under for a second time.

When he came to the surface once more, he had a terrible moment in which he could not find his son. Then he, too, reappeared. The captain later reported: "A most awful and heart-rending scene presented itself to my view; women and children struggling together amidst pieces of wreckage of every kind, calling on each other and God to assist them. Such another appalling scene may God preserve me from ever witnessing—I was in the act of trying to save my child when a portion of the paddlebox came crashing up edgewise and just grazed my head and fell with its whole weight on the head of my darling child. In another moment I beheld him a lifeless corpse on the surface of the waves."

Although the raft had been put together in the best possible way under the circumstances, it was not a perfect job. Seventy-two men and four women boarded it after the *Arctic* went down. Only one, Peter McCabe, managed to live through the following twenty-six-hour ordeal. Later, from the sanctuary of Sailors' Snug Harbor on Staten Island, New York, McCabe made the following statement:

"I swam to the large raft which had about seventy persons clinging to it. The sea, though not strong, was rough, and the waves, as they dashed over it, washed away a portion of its living freight. I shall never forget the awful scene. There we were, in the midst of the ocean, without the slightest hope of assistance, while every minute one or more of our unfortunate fellow passengers were dropping into their watery graves from sheer exhaustion. Those who had life preservers did not sink, but floated with their ghastly faces upward, reminding those who still remained alive of the fate that awaited them.

"In the midst of this, thank Heaven, I never lost hope, but retained my courage to the last. One by one I saw my unfortunate companions drop off; some of them floated off and were eaten and gnawed by fishes, while others were washed under the raft and remained with me till I was rescued. I could see their faces in the openings as they were swayed to and fro by the waves, which threatened every moment to wash me off. The raft at one time was so crowded that many had to hold on by one hand. Very few words were spoken by any, and the only sound that we heard was the splash of the waters or the heavy breathing of the poor sufferers as they tried to recover their breath after a wave had passed over them. Nearly all were submerged to their armpits, while a few could with great difficulty keep their heads above the surface.

"The women were the first to go. They were unable to stand the exposure more than three or four hours. They all fell off the raft without a word, except one poor girl who cried out in intense agony, 'Oh, my poor mother and sisters.'

"When I was about eighteen hours on the raft there were not more than three or four left. One of these gave me what appeared to be a small map, but which I understood him to say was a sort of title deed to his property. In a few minutes after I took it, he too unloosed his hold and was added to the number that floated about the raft.

"I endeavored to get the paper into my pocket, but found this impossible on account of my cramped position, so I placed it between my teeth and held it there till I was overwhelmed by a wave, when I lost my hold of it, and it was washed away. Another, who had an oiled silk coat on, called on me, for Heaven's sake, to assist him as his strength was rapidly failing and he must fall off if not relieved. As he was about four or five feet from me, it was difficult to reach him, but after considerable exertions I succeeded in doing so and helped him with one of my knees until I became quite faint, when I was obliged to leave him to his fate. Poor fellow, he promised me if he ever got to New York alive he would reward me well. He clung with terrible tenacity to life, but he too dropped off in his turn. I was now left alone on the raft; not a solitary being was alive out of seventy."

McCabe was eventually rescued by the ship *Huron* of St. Andrews, New Brunswick, bound for Quebec.

Henderson Moore, one of the passengers of the *Arctic*, had watched several others jump overboard into the water to get a place on one of the lifeboats. He was picked up by a lifeboat that had about fourteen people aboard. "We soon drifted out of sight of the steamer," Moore explained later. "After laying on our oars a few minutes, we went towards the steamer, being directed by the sound of her bells. While approaching her we fell in with another boat containing twenty-five persons in charge of the purser. Including those picked up, our boat now contained twenty-six persons in all, under the direction of Mr. Baalham. The boats being together, put it to vote and appointed him captain of both. We had at first six oars and the purser's boat three. We broke one of our oars and gave the purser one, which left us only four.

"We then headed for Cape Race, supposing it might be about a hundred miles distant, being guided by the wind and the sun which shone out for a few minutes. The compass taken on aboard failed to traverse and was of no use owing probably to the fact that Francis' lifeboats are made of iron. After pulling in company with the purser's boat all that night and the next day and night or until about one o'clock A.M. on the Friday following, we discovered land and which we reached about 4 P.M. the same day and landed at Broad Cove, a little bay and the only one within several miles where it was considered safe to effect a landing. Providentially a fisherman's hut was found near the spot, where we obtained some crackers and water, the first we had tasted after leaving the ship, as we had taken neither water nor food in either boat."

The first lifeboat to leave the *Arctic* vanished and was never heard from again.

The *Vesta* arrived at St. John's, Newfoundland, on September 30, just before the weather turned bad. At the time of the collision she had launched two lifeboats, one of which was run down by the *Arctic*. The other had returned to the ship, and its occupants were taken aboard again. Captain Duchesne of the *Vesta* had ordered 150 mattresses stuffed behind the bulkhead and fastened with timbers. The foremast was cut away and the vessel set out for St. John's under "small steam," according to the *Illustrated London News*.

One of the strangest consequences of the *Arctic* tragedy,

according to Alexander Crosby Brown, was the case of Mr. Fleury of New Orleans, who had supposedly perished on the liner. His young wife mourned for him and then married his chief clerk, by whom she had three children. Mr. Fleury had been taken aboard a whaler after the disaster and was then wrecked on an island, from which another whaler saved him. He finally arrived at New York six years later; on October 4, 1860, he wrote a letter to his wife.

Estimates as to the number saved and lost aboard the *Arctic* indicate the confusion common to this sort of statistics. Kennedy in *Steam Navigation* lists 87 saved of 365 on board. Angas in *Rivalry on the Atlantic* says 86 survived and 322 were lost. The U.S. Government reported that 305 disappeared. John G. Dow estimates that 106 were saved and 283 lost. Alexander Crosby Brown compiled a list of 83 saved from the *Arctic:* 4 officers, 57 crew members, 22 passengers; and one fisherman from the *Vesta.* Of course, the 11 men in the *Vesta*'s lifeboat must be added to the casualties.

No disciplinary action was taken against any of the survivors of the *Arctic,* some of whom had cowardly fought other men and even women to gain space in the lifeboats. Nevertheless, many of the surviving crew members decided to remain in Canada until the episode was dimmed by the passage of time and they could return home quietly without attracting attention. Alexander Crosby Brown relates that when Mr. W. W. Gilbert, a member of the New York Stock Exchange, arrived in New York alive and well, there was an "indescribable chill which ran through the entire community." In his own defense Gilbert said that he had gone to secure and hold seats for the lady members of the Brown family, but the inrush of the crew prevented him from getting out again. When he told his story it was believed that all witnesses who could contradict him had gone down with the ship. Later, George F. Allen, to the astonishment of all his friends, was picked up alive at sea. He did not confirm Mr. Gilbert's story, but what Mr. Allen did say was never made public.

When the crash occurred, Charles Mitchell, Sir Anthony's descendant, took momentary comfort in the realization that his sister Caroline was not aboard. Then the task of keeping alive occupied all his thoughts. He reached the ship's railing and grabbed a rope, from which he lowered himself and then jumped the remaining distance into the icy sea. Temporarily stunned by the fall, Mitchell was revived by the shock of the freezing water.

Feebly he swam to a lifeboat. Coming alongside, he was grasped by those aboard and hauled to safety. Minutes later the fog enveloped them, and they drifted away from the sinking ship. It was discovered that there were neither rations nor water aboard the lifeboat. There was no compass; they were adrift about forty-five miles from the nearest shore with no means of determining direction. During the next day two of the men gave in to their intense thirst and drank seawater; both died within twenty-four hours.

Two days later the fog lifted enough to allow the occupants of the lifeboat to see about a mile around them. Soon a schooner was sighted, but it sailed away without observing them. A brig came into view but also disappeared.

One of the crew then noticed what he believed was a land bird flying overhead. Assuming that it disappeared in the general direction of the shore, the occupants of the lifeboat started rowing after it. Hours later they landed at a small fishing village, Broad Cove, Newfoundland, twelve miles north of Cape Race.

Charles Mitchell was taken to the hut of a fisherman, where he had to remain for "a month before he recovered sufficiently from his exposure so that he could leave his benefactors and return to Charleston." *

* I have been permitted to quote from the pen of Mrs. S. Fahs Smith in recording the story of Charles Mitchell. Walter Ehrenfeld of York, Pennsylvania, also deserves special mention for making much of this chapter possible.

2

Blizzard
of '91

Unknown to most weather experts in the United States, in the year 1891 England suffered a blizzard of monumental proportions. The winter prior to the blizzard had been strange indeed. Europe was frozen from the Baltic to the Adriatic. Every major river of the Continent was blocked, and the port of Antwerp was closed by ice. The lakes of Zurich and Constance were frozen solid. Five inches of snow covered the streets of Naples. Then, on January 20, a sudden thaw occurred, the east wind turned westerly and the temperature went up to 40° F. Serious flooding resulted.

The great frost in England set in toward the end of November 1890. By Christmas the Serpentine in Hyde Park, the Welsh Harp at Hendon and the ponds around Hampstead and Highgate were covered with six inches of ice.

January 1891 remained cold, but February was characterized by fine, genial, springlike weather, so warm and dry that there was a drought in parts of Cornwall and Devon. Spring flowers bloomed and butterflies fluttered about. By the end of the month the *Royal Cornwall Gazette* reported that "agriculturalists have seldom had a fine February for spring sowings and seldom have they got so much grain into the ground by March 2nd, as they have this year."

With the arrival of March, the weather became unsettled but still remained dry. Friday, March 6, dawned fair, but the barometer was falling and it was getting colder. On Saturday much-needed rain fell fairly steadily until evening. By Sunday the cold front had moved south, although a small depression passing across the western counties of England caused frequent rain. During the night the wind changed from west to east, and throughout the day it strengthened and steadied at northeast. It became very cold, but still there was no anticipation of the unprecedented blizzard that was to come.

Monday, March 9, 1891, was fair. According to a contemporary report, "the barometer had been rising slightly, and . . . the day 'promised to be fine' . . . nothing was said about a great fall of snow, accompanied by a hurricane fierce enough to send it down in powder, without even allowing time for the formation of snowflakes."

By evening "the streets were deserted, all the traffic stopped; neither horse nor man could stand against the thick driving snow and the piercing wind." The blizzard of 1891 had arrived.

What made the storm a killer was not the snow itself but the easterly wind of hurricane force that rose at noon, March 9, and raged unabated until dusk the following day, making the snow fall "in blinding sheets . . . fine, powdery snow that . . . gradually piled up its tiny pellets into huge masses of a solid character many feet deep."

The blizzard claimed over two hundred lives, the majority at sea. Sixty-three ships foundered between the Goodwins and the Scilly Isles. Over half a million trees were brought down; many forests and woodlands took generations to recover.

Because of the suddenness of the storm, many farmers were caught with their flocks and herds up on the moors and high fields. In the driving wind it was impossible to round them up.

More than six thousand sheep and lambs were lost in Cornwall and Devon alone.

Incidentally, in 1891 *blizzard* itself was a new term, imported to England from the United States only a month before when a severe snowstorm was reported in Nebraska. The Union Pacific Railroad between Cheyenne, Wyoming, and Sydney, Nebraska, was blocked, and six mail or express trains with more than five hundred passengers were snowed in for two days. Little did anyone dream that the British railways would soon face similar conditions. Strangely enough, on the same March 9 another blizzard swept the states of Ohio, Illinois, Iowa and Minnesota.

It may behoove us all to be more wary than were those Englishmen on days our weather forecast reads as the *London Times* did that Monday, March 9, 1891: "North-easterly winds, moderate; fair generally."

3

Copper King
Thomas W. Lawson

In 1978 I wrote the history of the world's greatest schooner, the seven-masted *Thomas W. Lawson*. I used information from an interview with the last survivor of the *Lawson*, Engineer Edward Longfellow Rowe, shortly before his death. when the book * containing the *Lawson* chapter came out, I was amazed at the number of people anxious to obtain information about Thomas W. Lawson. This chapter explains more of the man himself and the reasoning behind his actions.

Probably there will never be another financial genius to equal Thomas W. Lawson, the so-called Yankee wizard of the stock market. Born in Charlestown, Massachusetts, in 1857, the son of Canadian parents, he spent his childhood in Cambridge. When twelve years old he ran away from school to obtain a position with a Boston investment firm; even at that tender age he was fascinated with the stock market.

Traced down, he was sent back to school. Within a short time he again escaped to Boston and got a job as an errand boy. This time his parents thought the matter over and allowed him to keep his position.

* *Adventures, Blizzards, and Coastal Calamities*, pp. 226−239.

When he reached the age of seventeen, Thomas Lawson began to show signs of the genius that was to make it possible for him to amass $53 million by 1900. He studied hard at home and concentrated on the intricate ways of the financial world, soon rising from errand boy to clerkship. At the age of eighteen he was installed as a clerk at the sedate Globe Bank of Boston. The next year he made a substantial killing in the stock market, then lost the relatively large sum by unfortunate manipulations within twenty-four hours.

Four years later the financial expert of twenty-two was actually established as an operator on "The Street." That same year he proposed marriage to Jeannie Augusta Goodwillie and was accepted.

At twenty-four Lawson began to sit at directors' tables in large corporations. He had made his first million dollars before reaching the age of thirty. A newspaper of that period states that Lawson was "a speculative factor of dominant influence, with a spirit of daring unusual, if not startling, in conservative Boston, and a surprising capacity for doing the seemingly impossible and the ultra sensational."

George Corliss, an inventive genius, believed Lawson would have been a great inventor if he had put all his energy into that particular field. "There is probably not another," said Corliss, "who possesses to such a marked degree the inventive genius combined with the thorough businessman; he is one of the very few who can quickly perceive the necessity for a new invention, who can make the invention, who can invent labor-saving machinery to produce the invention, who can manufacture that machinery, and who can then organize all these inventions into a business; and not only successfully conduct that business, but can personally interest all the capital which is necessary to make such a business a success."

When a lad in his teens Lawson invented a substitute for playing cards, which many held in disrepute. He soon put his game on the market and it had a long, successful run. Shortly after he was twenty he wrote, printed and produced a booklet on the national game of baseball.

During the Harrison-Cleveland presidential campaign of 1888, Lawson compiled and published more than 350,000 copies of his views on the Republican party leaders whom he favored. The Republicans were elected, although Lawson's part in the victory was said by some to have been relatively small.

Lawson's first great financial undertaking was successful reorganization of the Lawson Service Company. His second venture proved to be a disaster in a completely new field. Then he set Westinghouse Electric Company on its feet with several new inventions, making millions for himself as well.

Some time later he started dealings in copper stocks. He sold Butte and Boston stock short all the way down from $16 to 75 cents. Then he participated in reorganizing the company, being so successful that he became known as the Copper King.

As his wealth increased, he acquired a town house in Boston and a summer residence in Cohasset. By 1900 he was living in Winchester, and also occupying a large edifice on the water side of Boston's Beacon Street at Charlesgate East.

His property in Cohasset at the Dr. John Bryant estate consisted of about fifty acres. There he had stables for thirty-two horses and kennels for forty dogs. He also had magnificent gardens; in 1899 alone there were 15,000 cuttings, with 2800 hydrangeas stored in the stable cellar for the winter.

The story of the $30,000 pink carnation is a South Shore epic familiar to many people two or three generations ago. When Mrs. Lawson became an invalid shortly before the turn of the century, Thomas Lawson decided that only a particular type of carnation was worthy to decorate the rooms in which his wife now was forced to spend much of her time. The carnation was grown by Peter Fisher at Ellis in Norwood. Lawson bought the entire output for several years, then decided that it should be offered in competition with other flowers. The carnation was then named the "Mrs. Thomas W. Lawson Pink." It won a silver cup in the competition, the cup offered by Lawson himself.

In January 1899 Lawson competed with a Mr. Higgin-botham of Chicago for the right to own the pink. He offered $30,000 for eight thousand plants of the pink, an offer that was accepted. There has been controversy whether this trans-action ever took place. These are Mr. Lawson's own words of explanation: "I made my offer . . . on the spur of the moment, because I was touched by the pathos of the picture. In my mind's eye as I read of the Chicago and New York offers, I saw great circus posters blazoned with cabbages of a brilliant pink.

"And bye the bye, some of the dealers and growers say that no flower is worth what they term the extravagant price I have paid. Sentiment aside, I know a little something about flowers, and know considerable about carnations, and I will say to my critics that I can realize more than double the amount I have invested for my eight thousand plants.

"To anyone who can produce a finer carnation than 'The Mrs. Thomas W. Lawson' before February 1, I offer the sum of $5000."

The offer was never accepted, and the carnation, in the opinion of many Norwood growers, was never exceeded in beauty.

In 1899 Thomas Lawson added the 182-foot yacht *Dreamer* to his possessions. It was a splendid vessel, rich and tasteful in furnishings and decorations.

When he became interested in the America's Cup races, he became embroiled in a situation that was to divide yachtsmen all over the world into two camps.

The America's Cup was won at Cowes from an English fleet on August 22, 1851, by the yacht *America,* which had sailed across the ocean for the competition. The Cup has been ac-cepted as representing the world's blue ribbon of yachting. Thomas W. Lawson decided he would like to compete in the America's Cup Race in the 1901 season. On December 31, 1900, he ordered work to begin on a new sailing craft at the Atlantic Works in East Boston.

The keel of the new challenger, *Independence,* its base a

bronze casting made at East Braintree, was put in place on January 26, 1901. The vessel was fully in frame on March 6, and by April 25 all her body plates were in position so that burnishing could begin. The challenging craft was launched May 18, 1901, with full ceremony and great pride.

It was a tremendous blow to Lawson when he was informed that the *Independence* would not be allowed to compete for the right to meet the British challenger unless he joined the New York Yacht Club, which in all previous Cup races had represented the United States. The issue was basically whether anyone other than a member of the New York Yacht Club could compete for his country in defense of the America's Cup. After many arguments and bitter words, the New York Yacht Club ruled that "no American other than a member of the New York Yacht Club has the right to take part in the defense of an international cup."

Thomas Lawson was thus not allowed to compete. He issued the following statement: "My refusal, as owner of the American-built and American-named yacht *Independence,* to recognize the right of the custodians of the America's Cup to compel me, or any American, to join any club in order to compete for the honor of defending an American National trophy, led to this extraordinary ruling, which dazed the yachting world."

The sails of the *Independence* had been hoisted for the first time off Boston Light on June 3. On September 3 Lawson realized that the New Yorkers were not going to permit him to compete. With an admirable show of defiance, he lowered her sails for the last time in the same locality off America's oldest lighthouse. Wasting no time, Lawson began the work of breaking up the challenger at once; within a month she was reduced to a conglomerate pile of metal in a Lawley Yard boatshop.

Designer B. B. Crowninshield in 1902 surveyed with great pride Lawson's gigantic seven-masted schooner *Thomas W. Lawson,* launched that year at the Ship and Engine Building

Company in Quincy. Some people believe the magnificent craft was built to sail coal to Manila from this country—the *Thomas W. Lawson* did sail in the coal trade for almost four years. Then she was converted into a tanker, but her total effective service was limited to five years. This steel seven-master only had two rivals as a steel schooner; the six-masted *William L. Douglass* was the only one strictly New England-built.

In 1900 Thomas Lawson had become interested in moving into Scituate. There were several hundred undeveloped acres in the vicinity north and west of what is today called the Lawson Tower. He soon was visiting Scituate weekly, and at times daily, to make his plans for an unsurpassed estate. "Dreamwold," when completed, would make his name famous almost wherever the Massachusetts South Shore was mentioned.

Lawson succeeded far beyond his fondest dreams. Dreamwold was the most perfect example of its type in all eastern America. According to many Scituate residents, the only comparable place anywhere in the United States was Leland Stanford's great establishment across the country in California.

Dreamwold took many years to build, and during its construction the Town of Scituate erected a water tower that interfered with the pleasing panorama from the Lawson home.

Always a person to attempt to overcome difficulties whenever they presented themselves, Lawson at once visited the local water company and obtained permission to enclose the 153-foot tower with a wooden wall and conical roof. Thomas Lawson sent an architect to Europe to find an appropriate design that would be both attractive and historically correct in the tower and turret effect he wanted.

His ultimate choice was an edifice shaped like a Roman tower, with a separate turret at the side of the original water tower. The turret enclosed a spiral staircase of 123 steps that rose to a bell room in which were mounted ten bells. The bell ringer could operate the bells either from a music room on the ground floor or from the bell room itself.

Above the bell deck is a clock room in which a large clock used to strike the hours and play the Angelus automatically at seven in the morning and six at night. Nowadays, beginning in June, the custom of the Angelus is continued throughout the summer.

William Tecumseh Sherman, formerly of the Scituate Water Department, was responsible for the statement that the Lawson Tower, a New England landmark for mariners for years and years, is the most beautiful, most expensive, most photographed water tower in the entire United States.

Carol Miles, a librarian at the new Scituate Public Library, which is situated fairly near the Lawson Tower, told me that in 1907 Lawson wrote a book, *Friday the Thirteenth*. His daughter, Dorothy Lawson McCall, also wrote about her life in the book *The Copper King's Daughter*.

The turning point in Thomas W. Lawson's life probably occurred at the death of his wife, whom he adored. Jeannie Lawson died on August 5, 1906, and Lawson was never the same after that day. He did not noticeably lose his financial touch until several years later. It is said that his clash with the New York interests, involving the loss of millions of dollars, was the first indication that he was no longer the Tom Lawson of the turn of the century. His death on February 8, 1925, came only after he had lost almost his entire fortune.

4

Mary Had
a Little Lamb

Mary had a little lamb;
Its fleece was white as snow;
And everywhere that Mary went
The lamb was sure to go.

About fifteen years ago I took a canoe trip with several carries to a place near Sterling, Massachusetts, where stood the schoolhouse attended by Mary Sawyer, who had a little lamb. That trip aroused my interest in the nursery rhyme.

The story of the lamb was told by Mary herself when she was an elderly lady. I have here quoted from her whenever possible. For well over a century the story of Mary and her lamb has been repeated with various conclusions and opinions. I believe I can gain no further information by postponing the story and referring again to the various authors, locations and inferences.

"Well, if I had known," Mrs. Tyler smilingly said to a visitor at her home, "that the interest I took in my little pet was to have given me so much notoriety, I do not know that I should have carried out the plan I did; but I think I should, for then I was too young to understand about notoriety, though not too young to take an interest in dumb animals, especially when I saw them suffering."

At first Mrs. Tyler, formerly Mary Sawyer, was somewhat loath to talk for publication. But when informed that it was youngsters for whom the story was to be told, she related the tale as follows:

"I was always very fond of animals, and from the time I could toddle out to the barn I was with the dumb beasts not a little of my time. I think there was not a horse, cow, sheep, ox or any other animal upon the place but knew me. It was rare sport for me to pluck clover tops and make the horses follow me about the fields for them. By calling to them, or to the cows, I could get them to come to me, and I always intended to have something for them when they came.

"One cold, bleak March morning I went out to the barn with father. And after the cows had been fed, we went to the sheep pen and found two lambs that had been born in the night. One of them had been forsaken by its mother, and through neglect, cold and lack of food was nearly dead.

"I saw it had still a little life, and I asked to take it into the house. But father said, 'No, it is almost dead anyway, and at the best it may live but a short time.' I couldn't bear to see the poor little thing suffer, so I teased until I got it into the house. Then I worked upon mother's sympathies. At first the little creature could not swallow, and the catnip tea mother made, it could not take for a long time.

"I got the lamb warm by wrapping it in an old garment and holding it in my arms beside the fireplace. All day long I nursed the lamb, and at night it could swallow just a little. Oh, how pleased I was! But even then I wasn't sure it would live, so I sat up all night with it, fearing it wouldn't be warm enough if there was not someone at hand to look out for its comfort. In the morning, much to my girlish delight, it could stand. From that time it improved rapidly. It soon learned to drink milk, and from the time it could walk about, it would follow me anywhere if I only called it.

"My little pet was a fast grower, as symmetrical a sheep as ever walked, and its fleece was of the finest and whitest. I used to take as much care of my lamb as a mother would of a child. I washed it regularly, kept the burdocks picked out of its feet, and combed and trimmed with bright-colored ribbons the wool on its forehead. When that was being done, the lamb would hold down its head, shut its eyes and stand as quiet as could be.

"From the time it could walk until the season came for the sheep to go to pasture, my lamb stayed in the woodshed. It did not take kindly to its own species. When it was in the field, it preferred being with the cows and horses instead of with other sheep.

"The lamb was a ewe and became the mother of three lambs, a single one and twins. Her devotion to her little family was as strong as could be.

"We roamed the fields together, companions and fast friends. I did not have many playmates outside the dumb creatures on the place. There were not many little girls to play with, and I had few dolls. But I used to dress up my lamb in pantalets, and had no end of pleasure in her company. Then I had a little blanket or shawl for her; usually when that was on, she would lie down at my feet, remaining perfectly quiet and seemingly quite contented.

"The day the lamb went to school, I hadn't seen her before starting off. Not wanting to go without seeing her, I called. She recognized my voice, and soon I heard a faint bleating far down the field. More and more distinctly I heard it, and I knew my pet was coming to greet me. My brother Nate said, 'Let's take the lamb to school with us.'

"Childlike, I thought that would be a good idea, and quickly consented. The lamb followed along close behind me. There was a high stone wall to climb, and it was rather hard work to get her over. We got her on top, then clambered over to take her down. She seemed to understand what was expected, and waited quietly for us to take her off the wall.

"When the schoolhouse was reached, the teacher had not arrived, and but few of the scholars were there. Then I began to think what I should do with the lamb while school was in session. I took her down to my seat—we had old-fashioned high boarded-up seats then. Well, I put the lamb under the seat and covered her with her blanket. She lay down as quietly as could be. By and by I went forward to recite, leaving the lamb all right. But in a moment there was a clatter, clatter, clatter on the floor, and I knew it was the pattering of the hoofs of my lamb.

"Oh, how mortified I felt! The teacher was Miss Polly Kimball, who was afterward married to a Mr. Loring and became the mother of Loring, the circulating-library man of Boston. She laughed outright, and of course all the children giggled. It was rare sport for them, but I could see nothing amusing in the situation. I was too ashamed to laugh, or even smile, at the unlooked-for appearance of my pet. I took her outdoors and shut her in a shed until I was ready to go home at noon. Usually I did not go home till evening, for we carried our lunch with us; but I went home at noon that day.

"Visiting the school that morning was a young man by the name of John Roulstone, a nephew of the Reverend Lemuel Capen, who was then settled in Sterling. It was the custom then for students to fit for college with ministers, and for this purpose Mr. Roulstone was studying with his uncle. The young man was very much pleased with the incident of the lamb. The next day he rode across the fields on horseback to the little old schoolhouse and handed me a slip of paper, which had written upon it the three original stanzas of the poem. Since then three additional stanzas have been added to it. Here is the little poem as I received it:

> Mary had a little lamb;
>   Its fleece was white as snow;
> And everywhere that Mary went,
>   The lamb was sure to go.

It followed her to school one day,
   Which was against the rule;
It made the children laugh and play
   To see a lamb at school.

And so the teacher turned it out;
   But still it lingered near,
And waited patiently about
   Till Mary did appear.

"From the fleece sheared from my lamb, mother knit two pairs of very nice stockings, which for years I kept in memory of my pet. But when the ladies were raising money for the preservation of the Old South Church in Boston, I was asked to contribute one pair of these stockings for the benefit of the fund. This I did. The stockings were raveled out, pieces of the yarn being fastened to cards bearing my autograph, and these cards were sold, the whole realizing, I am told, about one hundred dollars. After the first pair were thus sold, the ladies wanted more yarn. They were so anxious to have the other pair raveled out, that I gave them also. Now all I have left in remembrance of my little pet of years long ago is two cards, upon which are pasted scraps of the yarn from which the stockings were knit.

"I have not told you about the death of my playmate. It occurred on a Thanksgiving morning. We were all out in the barn, where the lamb had followed me. It ran right in front of the cows fastened in the stanchions, running along the feed-box. One of the creatures gave its head a toss, then lowered its horns and gored my lamb, which gave an agonizing bleat and came toward me with blood streaming from its side. I took it in my arms, placed its head in my lap and there it bled to death. During its dying moments it would turn its little head and look up into my face in a most appealing manner, as if it would ask if there was not something that I could do for it. It was a sorrowful moment for me when the companion of many of my romps, my playfellow of many a long summer's day, gave up its life. Its place could not be filled in my childish heart."

Mrs. Annie E. Sawyer, Mary's niece and a Somerville schoolteacher, made Mary's declining years peaceful and happy. Mary died December 11, 1889, and is buried in Mount Auburn Cemetery.

Henry S. Sawyer deposes and says:

That he is a relative of Mary E. Tyler, née Sawyer, deceased; that he lives in the same house in which she was born and married, and in which she lived at the time the incidents referred to in the poem of "Mary Had a Little Lamb" occurred. That he attended school at the same schoolhouse where she attended school at the time referred to in the poem, and that he knows the facts as published here to be true.

Henry S. Sawyer

Sworn and subscribed before me, a Notary Public in and for the Commonwealth of Massachusetts, this sixth day of May, A.D. one thousand nine hundred and one.

William A. Wilcox
Notary Public

Several incidents or stories that have developed during the years should be told in this chapter. In 1927 a large gathering of friends met at Llangollen, Wales, to celebrate the eighty-sixth birthday of Mrs. Mary Hughes. She tells us that her father, John Thomas, had a pet lamb named Billy that went to school with Mrs. Hughes, and was removed by the teacher as he had "frisked and gamboled about the room in a way to cause a commotion among the children." In some way Sarah Josepha Hale of Newport, New Hampshire, toured Wales in 1849 and immediately wrote the nursery rhyme that included the following stanza:

> And you each gentle animal
> In confidence may bind,
> And make them follow at your call
> If you are always kind.

In December 1931 Mrs. Hughes died in Worthing, England. Senator Horatio Hale, who married Sarah Buel, was staying with the Hughes family at Ty Issa Farm in Vale Llangollen, North Wales. Miss Buel set the lamb incident in verse.

Sarah Josepha Buell Hale, who was just mentioned but with a slightly different spelling of her middle name, was born in 1788 and died in 1879. Without Mrs. Hale, Bunker Hill Monument never would have been finished. In the *Ladies Magazine* she began her active literary life, writing about half of each issue herself. She initiated the Seaman's Aid Society and raised enough money to finish the laggard plans for Bunker Hill Monument, for which work she should receive full credit. Her magazine for women provided a periodical that was "a beacon-light of refined taste, pure morals, and practical wisdom."

Late in life her part in the "Mary Had a Little Lamb" story was told to her son, and she stated to him that she had written the volume, as is explained in *Century* for March 1904. Nevertheless, she does not mention Mary and her lamb specifically, and she titled the book *Poems for Our Children* (it was reprinted in 1916). It is believed that she wrote the last three stanzas of the nursery rhyme.

There are four people in the last twenty years who have written me concerning Mary. Mrs. George Walker writes that the school was moved and is now located on the Wayside Inn estate. Larayne Gallagher says that the school was rebuilt and still has "the same desks, stove, etc. as it had originally." I also heard from Sarah Jacobus, Mary's great-aunt, and from Miss Amy Stone, whose father's relatives recalled Mrs. Tyler selling yarn from the lamb's wool.

5

The *Portland* Legacy

When the first piercing winds of a chill November gale swirl into the harbors and inlets along the New England coast, the thoughts of many mariners turn to the night in 1898 when the *Portland* sailed out of Boston Harbor, never to return.

The *Portland* left Boston on Saturday evening, November 26, 1898, on her regular trip to Maine. As she backed out from India Wharf, it was beginning to snow. Later that evening, during the snowstorm, she was seen by men at Thacher's Island, off Cape Ann, and was also sighted by sailors aboard four different vessels in the vicinity. The storm soon became a hurricane, and the great seas probably disabled the *Portland,* battering and pushing her across Massachusetts Bay toward Cape Cod.

Early the next morning Captain Samuel Fisher of the Race Point Life Saving Station at Cape Cod heard several blasts from a steamer's whistle. Later that morning the weather changed completely and the sun came out for a short time. It was then that District Superintendent Benjamin C. Sparrow noticed two steamers and a fishing schooner off the Cape Cod shore. The fishing schooner was the *Ruth M. Martin,* whose captain, Michael Francis Hogan, was steering his damaged craft under jury rig for Provincetown Harbor, which he reached some hours later.

Around eleven o'clock that morning the storm shut in again and, a short time later, was as severe as before. Evidence points to the foundering of the *Portland* at a point five miles northeast of the High Head Life Saving Station on Cape Cod that Sunday evening at about 9:30. Watches found later on the victims were stopped between half-past nine and ten o'clock. Not one of the 191 persons aboard the ship ever reached shore alive to tell his story of horror. Wreckage began to come up on the great Cape Cod beach as early as seven o'clock that evening; by Monday morning the shore was littered with debris for miles in each direction. Thirty-six bodies were recovered from the wreck of the *Portland*.

On July 1, 1945, Diver Al George, working on a clue I received from Captain Charles L. Carver of Rockland, Maine, located the *Portland* in 144 feet of water 7½ miles out to sea from Race Point Coast Guard Station. He brought up a key from one of the staterooms, plainly marked PORTLAND. His words follow:

"It would seem as though the *Portland* had hit bottom on her beam ends and then through the years had worked her way into the sand until she is buried almost completely. Only the bare hull of the ship seems in position.

"All superstructure evidently has been spread around the ocean bed long ago. The boulders are much higher than my head. I could not tell whether I had found the foremast or the mainmast. Going down on my hands and knees, I could make out the ripples of sand on the bottom of the sea and could see little shells from time to time.

"It was a strange experience standing there alone with the ill-fated *Portland* and probably what remained of the passengers and crew still imprisoned in her sand-covered hull."

Part Five

1900–1940

1

The Chelsea Fire
of 1908

On Palm Sunday, April 12, 1908, a group of us who had been attending Sunday School in Winthrop, Massachusetts, were returning home to various parts of Cottage Hill, where the Winthrop water tower stands today. We all separated at the fire alarm box at the corner of Cottage and Hillside avenues, where I lived.

Suddenly as we were calling out farewells we saw a great yellowish-brown, funnel-shaped cloud of smoke in the air. It crossed diagonally over Cottage Avenue, about 150 yards to the west of us, near the Harrison Gray Otis estate. We ran to the area where the billowing clouds were rushing through the sky at more than a mile a minute.

A moment later, as we looked upward, we were astonished to see a good-size fragment of wood in the midst of the smoking funnel, being carried along toward the sea. I have never forgotten that wooden timber, which must have weighed three or four pounds, so high in the sky above us.

The following story by William J. McClintock is presented here through the kindness of Helen J. McClintock, his daughter.

"I am going to take you back to April 12, 1908, in my old home city of Chelsea, Massachusetts. It was Palm Sunday—a beautiful day in the spring, but with a fifty- or sixty-mile gale blowing from the west.

"Many residents were preparing to attend services in their various places of worship, not dreaming that within the next few terrifying hours our city would be reduced to rubble and ruin by one of the greatest fires ever to occur in this country. I was then a resident of Chelsea, and it was my privilege to witness events from the actual start of the fire, through the next twelve hours and for two weeks on relief work. Because of the terrific speed and widespread action of this event, no one person could possibly have seen it all. The following is simply a story of my own experiences and observations during those twelve terrifying hours.

"Shortly after ten on that memorable morning, an alarm of fire sounded. Now, I belonged to that great fraternity called 'sparks,' and we loved to 'follow the engines.' There were several box numbers that did not merit our attention. This was one of them. However, upon looking out my window and seeing a cloud of smoke scudding along with the gale, I decided to go. The fire was about a mile from my house in a small wooden factory which was pretty badly burned. The firemen had responded in good time, and in spite of the gale had 'knocked the fire down.' Some of the apparatus had returned to quarters. One hose company was standing by, 'playing a stream' on the ruins as a precautionary measure. The last engine company was preparing to leave. As there did not seem to be any further excitement, I started for home. Meeting a friend, we walked along together.

"About one hundred yards from the original fire, and to the north, was a comparatively new wooden building. . . . As we rounded the corner and crossed the street, I glanced at this building, noticed a peculiar orange-red glow in the second-story window and called my friend's attention to it. . . .

"At that moment a small wisp of smoke issued from the side

of one of the windows. We decided that the building was on fire. I started for the nearby box to pull in the alarm just as Engine 3 rounded the corner on the way back to its station. I stopped it and told the driver that I thought the building was on fire. . . . Turning to his engineer, he shouted, 'Blow your whistle and call that hose wagon back. . . .'

"The hose wagon returned with only two or three men on it, as many of the call men had gone home by horse and carriage or bicycle. I told the captain of our discovery and they started to throw the hose out into the street. Now, when this hose was picked up at the original fire, it was disconnected, rolled into coils and thrown loosely into the wagon. This all had to be made up into a single line. They were shorthanded so we pitched in to help. . . .

"At this moment Chief Spencer arrived. More smoke was appearing now. He sent a man to pull in the alarm. The hoseman was alone at the pipe, so I gave him a hand. He shouted, 'Play away three,' the old-time call for the water to be turned on. We directed the stream, and when the water hit one of the windows there was a muffled explosion caused by the accumulated gas and hot air. All the windows were blown out. Blazing rags from the factory, borne by the gale, soon filled the air and headed toward home. We could see them landing on roofs, in dry grass, in litter. The Chelsea fire had started on its way.

"Now Chief Spencer had always dreaded the conditions which existed on that day—an outside fire, a strong wind in the right direction and acres of shingled roofs, tinder dry. He immediately sent a messenger to Police Headquarters with the request that they call Boston for help as quickly as possible, for a conflagration threatened.

"Local apparatus and men were now returning . . . and I was soon relieved from my duty on the pipe. It was not long before several streams were working on blazing roofs, dry grass, paper and other litter. As fast as one fire was put out, others started.

"My friends and I started up toward town. There was confusion everywhere. People were beginning to move furniture and household goods out into the street. They were crying, screaming, looking for lost children, relatives and pets. Nobody seemed to know what to do or how to do it. We stopped at numerous houses to warn residents to seek safety. As many of these people did not speak our language, we had difficulty with them. In one such situation, with the roof afire, we had to forcibly drag an elderly couple out of the house. A neighbor took them in charge.

"The call for outside help was now being answered and apparatus was coming from several directions. Fires were so widely scattered that a central command was impossible. Each company arriving on the scene had to select a position best suited for conditions. Some streets were so blocked with household goods that apparatus could not get through.

"With help pouring into the city, it now seemed possible that the fire might be checked. But with the strong gale that was blowing, these hopes gradually faded. The fire was making great jumps and the people were in a state of panic. As street after street burst into flames, it became certain no human force could stop the fire.

"I arrived at the corner of Chestnut and Fourth streets in front of the Universalist Church where the Reverend Mr. R. Perry Bush was standing on the steps with some parishioners. He asked me what the prospects were. I told him they were very bad, and if he had any valuables inside which he would save, he had better get them out and leave in a hurry. I then went up into the steeple to observe the fire from there. When I arrived on the bell deck, the wind was terrific. The last time I saw my hat it was sailing over the rooftops. Flames were leaping in great tongues, smoke was thick, sparks and embers were falling in showers and the heat was intense. It was an ominous sight.

"At this time a Boston fire company stopped at the corner. They had seen a fire on the roof of a house directly behind the church and stopped to take care of it. I had no hat, so I borrowed a fire helmet from the wagon and started to help the firemen. There was a ladder against the house, which we used to take care of the fire. We soon extinguished it.

"Two elderly women stood at the corner opposite the church. I went to them, warned them of the danger and advised them to leave for safety. One of them said she could not go until her husband returned. It seemed that he was out with his wagon helping some friends move goods from the danger zone. He never returned. He was one of the seventeen known victims. . . . The two women were taken to the Cary Avenue Church for safety.

"I went down Fourth Street to Broadway, which was alive with excitement. Businessmen were trying to save goods, fire engines were at work and streams of water were wetting down the buildings. . . . The fire had not taken hold of Broadway but had jumped several blocks and was raging in Division and Hawthorne streets.

"I arrived at Bellingham Square and stood talking to a policeman as we looked up Hawthorne Street, a roaring mass of fire and smoke. As we watched, a flaming board came out of the smoke like an arrow and pierced the roof of a house. I was interested to know how long this house would last so I timed it. In eighteen minutes there was nothing left.

"During this period there suddenly appeared out of that seething mass of smoke and fire a fire engine, horses galloping. It was then that I saw demonstrated the affection old-time drivers had for the animals in their care. The man got down from his seat, went around and hurriedly examined the horses to see if they were injured and burned. He stroked them and hugged them around the neck as much as to say, 'Boys, you saved our lives.'

"From here I went down to the common, now called Union Park, about two blocks away. This was a small area covering a city block, planted with grass and trees and adjacent to the Boston & Maine Railroad, which up to then had served as a barrier to help keep the fire from the northern part of the city. This park, like all other vacant spots, was piled high with household goods; even a few carriages and two or three horses were tied to trees.

"At a time like this one may see human nature in many of its moods: sorrow, terror, fright, panic—even comedy. These manifestations appeared in so many cases that to enumerate them all would be impossible. At one point a Negro preacher stood on a box loudly calling upon the Almighty to stop the fire. Not far away a local character, noted for his Shakespearean endeavors, removed his hat and cried, 'Burn on ye fiery demon, burn on. . . .'

"The streets were full of refugees. Everybody was carrying something—articles of value and some of doubtful worth—apparently the first thing that was snatched up when they were suddenly driven from their homes. I saw one man carrying a parrot cage containing a very frightened cat. Another carried an empty tin pail, and another embraced an armful of framed pictures.

"The fire had now been raging for about two hours. It had jumped to Bellingham Hill and had started to attack the oil tanks in East Boston. Gradually the engines were forced out of the fire zone.

"About this time I returned home. It was not until then that my wife learned that part of Chelsea was in ashes. After a consultation we packed a few necessities and closed our house. Through the kindness of a neighbor, my wife and the baby were driven to her parents' home in Everett until conditions for housekeeping were more favorable. I went up onto Powderhorn Hill with a camera and got a panoramic view of the fire from there.

"I returned home and was about to pick up a lunch when a messenger arrived from my father with a request for the loan of my fire extinguisher. There were a few doughnuts and cookies in the pantry which I tucked in my pocket, and taking the extinguisher, I returned with the messenger. On the way back I laughed out loud when I thought of my puny extinguisher going to face that roaring inferno ahead.

"My father's house was not in direct line of the fire. It was on the north side of the railroad opposite St. Rose Church buildings. When I arrived a squad of soldiers had just finished tearing down the wooden fence along the railroad location. One of my brothers was in the cupola on the stable with a supply of water; another brother with a group of friends and other volunteers was deployed along the railroad bank with water, brooms and other equipment, watching for any stray spark that might cross the very important safety zone. There did not appear to be anything to do at the moment, so I sat down on my pony tank and ate doughnuts and cookies. This was my Sunday supper.

"The fire was now coming up Chestnut Pocket, a dead-end street stopping at the railroad. This was a crucial spot now and the fire-fighting forces, concentrated on the Washington Avenue and Broadway bridges, were making a desperate stand to keep the fire from crossing the railroad. . . . The armory, St. Rose Convent and school were in flames, and St. Rose Church was beginning to burn. Across Broadway the car barns of the Boston Elevated Railway were in flames. Adjacent to them across Gerrish Avenue, Cobb's Livery Stable was being deluged by several streams of water, with the result that only one corner containing the office was burned. The car barns were destroyed. . . .

"My father's house was a busy place. Several of his friends who had been burned out had sought refuge there. . . . My brother, a practicing physician, had an office adjacent to the house, and this too was a scene of activity. A continuous line of policemen, firemen, soldiers and others came in for emergency treatment of burns, cuts and other injuries. All serious cases were sent to the hospital at the Soldiers' Home.

". . . In the latter part of the afternoon the wind abated. The fire in Chelsea was practically under control, although it was still raging among the oil tanks, bridges, pumping station and other buildings in East Boston. The fire-fighting forces now massed along the perimeter of the fire were striving to extinguish the last remaining threat. There was an intermittent screaming of whistles as engines called for more coal. There were thirty-nine engines at work in Chelsea on that day, three of which were trapped by the fire, abandoned and destroyed.

"Seventeen thousand people had been burned out of their homes. Many of them had been taken in by the more fortunate. Others were being sheltered in the few remaining schools and churches. Many were in tents brought in by the Army and the Red Cross. The great majority, however, had left town to be with relatives or friends. Army kitchens were being rushed in to feed the soldiers and refugees.

"In the evening a group of city officials and prominent citizens met in the high school for the purpose of formulating relief plans. This meeting was held by light of kerosene lanterns sent in by a neighboring city's highway department. A committee was organized and started to work immediately. Food and clothing were needed at once, and a call was sent out for these supplies.

"At two o'clock that morning, I stood in a window of the high school and saw the last building burn in Chelsea. I could see two or three illuminated spots in the sky and could hear the distant humming of the engines as the last remaining fires were being extinguished. The continual roar and whistling of the pumps had been gradually diminishing since late afternoon. Much of the apparatus had returned to their home stations. The city was now in darkness and comparative quiet, as if exhausted from its stunning blow.

"Shortly after this my father, who had been selected as chairman of the relief committee, requested that I accompany him to the courthouse on the southerly side of the burned area. We found a military guard posted along the edges of the area, with orders not to allow anyone through. We were trying in vain to explain our mission when Captain Whiting, in charge of that detail, appeared on the scene. As he could vouch for us, we received permission to enter. However, he insisted on a military escort, for the sentries had received orders to shoot, if necessary, anyone ignoring the order to stay away.

"We started out on what proved to be a weird trip. There was no light except that shed by the kerosene lantern that I bore. The pavement, mostly of granite blocks, was still uncomfortably hot in places, littered with rubble and other noncombustible material and a tangle of wires of all sizes. My father was a former city engineer, and he and I had roamed the streets for thirty years. But we were lost in that utter desolation. We finally reached the courthouse. Our errand completed, we started the return trip over the same route. We were challenged at the sentry line, but our escort finally convinced the sentry that everything was in order and we continued the trip. The remains of numerous coal piles in cellar holes were burning, some of the gas pipes in the cellars were still emitting flames and there was a faint sound of water from broken pipes. The gas from the burning coal and the dust was choking in that awesome stillness. As we approached the ruins of City Hall, we were again challenged by two men in uniform. One of them proved to be Captain Whiting, who quickly let us through so that we could return home.

"The call for food and clothing had been spontaneously answered, and these necessities were now coming into the high school. Bread lines were formed and people waited patiently in line for this welcome commodity. I saw one bread line nearly half a mile long. A corps of volunteers were kept busy unpacking, sorting and dispensing these goods.

"A stupendous task now faced the city and public utilities. The fire had caused complete destruction. Hundreds of water and gas service pipes had to be shut off, sewer connections attended to, streets cleared, fire and police signal systems restored, and dangerous walls torn down. The telephone, electric and street railway companies lost all their wires, poles, meters and telephones. Heat was so intense that wooden poles were burned two feet down into the ground. Early Monday morning crews of workers arrived to start this task. Many of them came from distant points. A military guard was surrounding the area with sentries, patrolling within that line to keep all unauthorized persons out in order that the work would not be impeded. Chelsea had started on the road to recovery.

"I'm going to give a few statistics in order to show the enormous destruction wrought by this disaster. There were 490 acres burned over, more than three thousand shade trees were destroyed and most of the granite curbing in the city was ruined, seven hundred business and professional men were burned out and two bridges were destroyed. Seventeen persons lost their lives, the majority of these being trapped by the fire. Among the public and other buildings destroyed were the City Hall, the Board of Health, eight schools, thirteen churches, Frost General Hospital, two fire stations, the public library, armory, Masonic Temple, Post Office, Y.M.C.A., three bank buildings and four newspaper plants. The insurance losses paid amounted to approximately $8,840,000."

The following excerpts are from a letter written by Paul McClintock, son of the first writer.

"At 10:30 A.M. the fire alarm rang, and Frank [his chum] and I went down to see the fire. Our way led us along the B & M R.R. track toward Everett. The wind blew a gale, and looking ahead was almost impossible, on account of things flying in the air. We walked three fourths of a mile up to the fire.

"It was not a very exciting fire, for the firemen kept the flames inside, and so in about twenty minutes we walked around to the other side to see if anything was doing there. We had been standing directly to windward before, and the smoke hid everything from sight to leeward. But when we reached the tracks again to one side, we were surprised to see a big three-story rag shop, six hundred feet down the line, ablaze all over, and in a minute one wall had burned through and fallen in.

"Five hundred feet from this new fire, and about the same distance from the original one, another and much larger rag shop was covered with flames, and things began to look interesting.

"The continual calls on the fire alarm finally brought engines from Boston (about nineteen), Malden, Melrose, Saugus, Somerville, Medford, Lynn and possibly other places.

"I ran back home to get a camera, but mine was out at Tufts, Sam's was not to be found and there was only one in the whole house—the little Brownie of Sam's that had a film in it two years old I guess. I was mad at that, for the smoke was making a beautiful sight, and the flames could be plainly seen from our house. However, I took what I had to and ran back to the Boston Blacking Company's plant (where it started) and passed through the smoke to the other side of the fire from the house.

"By that time there were about eighteen buildings going (that I was aware of). The wind was carrying huge sparks through the air, spreading the fire almost as fast as one could walk. I walked toward Chelsea Square as far as Fourth Street, where I turned up and walked up Everett Avenue toward the fire again.

"Very soon I passed the fire line and struck a dense stream of smoke so black that I had to use my handkerchief (which was black with pitch) to breathe with, and trust to my knowledge of the street and my sense of direction to tell where I was. After I once got in I was not so sure about getting out, but finally I did and stood in the shelter for a moment to cool off and get some fresh air. My clothes were so hot I thought they were on fire. The smoke hid everything so I could take no pictures, and I started for home again to leave my camera and put on old clothes so I could get into the game and be of some help.

"From each house and tenement articles of cheap furniture

were being carried out and piled on the sidewalk, where, if it belonged to someone fortunate to have a horse at his disposal, it was carted away, or else left to be burned. As I passed by Union Square I saw it being filled with all kinds of furniture, none of which was destined to be saved.

"At home I went up to the billiard room (third floor) where I took in the situation. The course of the nearer edge of the fire seemed directed toward Bellingham Square, or slightly this side of it. But even though we seemed to be out of danger, a change of five degrees in the wind would have settled our fate without argument.

"I kept one eye on the progress of the fire. It had crept up Chestnut Street and up Broadway, settling on the large Catholic Church one hundred feet from us. The church was a brick edifice with a slate roof, as was the convent and the school next to it. I had taken up my post on the stable roof and had a large rope made fast to the cupola, by which I could cover the whole roof. The house and stable are both slate-roofed, but the wooden cupola and wooden walls were excellent places for a fire to get a foothold.

"I could look down on the railroad, and I saw a train of flatcars being filled with all kinds of articles. Lying across two rails was a piano with the legs unscrewed. I learned later that almost all this assortment belonged to the Blisses.

"The church kept blazing up until my position was too warm for comfort. The woodwork was almost unbearably hot, and the wind, the strongest I ever experienced, made it hard to wet the hot woodwork, because it blew the water right out of the saucepan I was using. Just then I looked toward Everett and saw that the fire had crossed the tracks and all indications pointed toward our being driven out in a short space of time.

"I looked on the other side, and there was the nozzle of a hose pointing at me. I thought it was time for me to vacate, so I climbed down. The yard was full of people. I followed up the hose to see where it came from. It led toward an engine on the corner of Lawrence Street and Clark Avenue, but stopped fifty feet short because of scarcity of hose.

"I went back to the house, where I learned that Bliss's house was gone. None of us expected to remain long where we were, but soon the church began to burn out, and in twenty minutes we were assured that all danger was past. (I then thought it was about one o'clock, but on looking at the clock saw it was five-thirty.)

"Had the fire in Fairfield's place, near Spruce Street on this side of the railroad, not been controlled, probably twice as many houses, including our own, would have gone. But a hard fight was put up there, and a successful one. We did escape, but it was a mighty close call. I thought they might dynamite our house to save the section this side of the track. I did, in fact, give the people warning, at one time, that they would have five minutes to get out with what they wanted.

"Around six o'clock we made about fifty sandwiches and over a gallon of coffee for the firemen and soldiers, who had arrived early at the scene of the fire. Most of us had eaten nothing since eight-thirty, but excitement killed our appetites.

"That night I learned that Raymond Bliss had saved almost all of his furniture. A train of flatcars backed from Revere to where it could be loaded with things to be saved, but strangely enough the Blisses were about the only ones to profit by it. There was a small army of people in the Bliss house ready to help, and Raymond, by judicious management, got them to take almost everything out that he wanted, without breaking anything to speak of. The train was pulled to Revere, where Raymond and I shortly went with a wagon and removed the furniture to our stable. We got two double-horse loads that night, and got in bed by two. At six we were up and made another load. The amount they saved in so short a time was wonderful."

2

Hermit Mason Walton

More than two thirds of a century ago a man by the name of Mason Walton was slowly wearing away because of his unsuccessful bouts with civilization. Deciding to do something about it, he eventually moved from his home in Boston to Cape Ann.

The world has not heard much about Mason Walton, although in my opinion his writing puts him in a class with Henry David Thoreau and John Burroughs. Some of his thoughts, penned in 1903, follow.

"Eighteen years ago I was in sore straits. Ill health had reduced my flesh until I resembled the living skeleton of a dime show. I realized that a few months more of city life would take me beyond the living stage, and that the world would have no further use for me except to adorn some scientific laboratory.

"A diagnosis of my case would read as follows: Dyspepsia, aggravated, medicine could give but slight relief. Catarrh, malignant, persistent. A douche was necessary every morning to relieve the severe facial pain. A cough that had worried me by day and by night, and thrived on all kinds of cough medicine. Also my lungs were sore and the palms of my hands

154

were hot and dry. I thought that I was fading away with consumption, but the doctors said my lungs were sound. I was advised to go into the woods and try life in a pine grove. As there was no money for the doctors in this advice, I looked upon it as kind and disinterested, but my mind ran in another direction.

"When I was young and full of notions, the idea entered my head that I should like a change from fresh to salt water. It resulted in a two months' trip on a fishing schooner. During the trip I had been free from seasickness, and had gained flesh rapidly. The memory of that sea voyage haunted me, now that I had become sick and discouraged. It seemed to me that a few weeks on salt water would save my life.

"With high hopes I boarded the little steamer that plied between Boston and Gloucester. I thought it would be an easy matter to secure board on one of the many vessels that made short trips after mackerel. For three days I haunted the wharves in vain. The 'skippers,' one and all, gave the same reason for refusing my offers. 'We are going after fish,' said they, 'and cannot be bothered with a sick man.' At last one 'skipper' discouraged me completely. He said to me, 'I once took a sick man on board, and because we did not strike fish, the fishermen called the passenger a Jonah, and made his life miserable. Three days after we returned he died, and I swore then that I never would take a sick man to sea.' This 'skipper's' story, and my fruitless efforts, caused me to abandon the salt water cure. I turned now to the hills around Gloucester. In the end I selected Bond's Hill, because it was surrounded by pine groves.

"I found the hill covered with blueberry and huckleberry bushes, the latter loaded with fruit. On the brow of the hill the soil had been washed away, leaving great masses of bed rock (granite) towering above the cottages that clung to the base of the cliff. On the extreme brow of the hill I found a spot where the soil had gathered and maintained a grass plot. Here I pitched my little tent. Here I lived from August to December. I called the spot the Eyrie, because it reminded me of the regions inhabited by eagles. A visit to the spot will disclose the fitness of the name."

On this spot eighteen years of hermit life began for Mason Walton. At first he made it a practice to go to town every day for one meal, bringing back supplies enough to last until another day. But he soon found the huckleberries, crab apples and occasional grapes good wholesome food that did not aggravate his chronic dyspepsia.

Two weeks of outdoor life brought a little more color to Walton's cheeks and made him feel like a new man. About this time he awoke one morning to realize that he had not coughed during the night. The cough that had harassed him night and day for two years left then and there, never to return. Before long his other complaints were also gone.

From his Eyrie, Walton looked out over the panorama, entranced with the ebb and flow of the tide through the marshes, the view of the outer harbor with its variety of fishing craft, and the city of Gloucester sprawling out across the way to Magnolia and Manchester. There, too, was Dogtown Common,* a boulder-covered region of pasture land choked by huckleberry and blueberry bushes.

Sunsets seen from the Eyrie were often beautiful beyond description. Whenever a massive bank of clouds hung above the western horizon, the setting sun illuminated the city from Riverdale to Eastern Point, and every window in sight glowed like burnished gold. Such glorious moments contributed a sense of well-being that Walton had never known before.

Well satisfied with his new way of life at Cape Ann, Walton constructed a substantial hut in a clearing. One April morning he found a flock of fox sparrows in the dooryard. It is more than unusual that for the three years following they reappeared on the same day of the month. On April 2, 1887, the

* See my 1978 book *Adventures, Blizzards, and Coastal Calamities*, p. 240.

hermit awoke early to find three feet of snow in the dooryard, and he was obliged to shovel the snow away in order to feed his good friends the sparrows on bare ground.

Mason Walton describes the bird as follows:

"The fox-sparrow is two-thirds as large as a robin, and may be classed with the beautiful birds both in form and coloration. The sexes are alike. The color above is a rich rusty red, deepest and brightest on the wings, tail, and rump. The head, neck, and shoulders are a dark ash color, more or less streaked with rusty red. Below the groundwork is snow-white, also thickly spotted with rust red. It could be called a wood-thrush by a careless observer. These birds are migrants with us, and pass through the State to their breeding grounds in April, to return in October. It is usually six weeks from the time the first flock appears before the loiterers are all gone. The flock that called on me was a very large one, numbering over a hundred birds. Mornings they made the woods ring with their delightful music."

With the coming of spring, Walton found that he was a trespasser on the nesting grounds of many woodland birds. Robins, thrushes, towhee-buntings, catbirds and numerous warblers nested around his cabin.

By this time Mason Walton had settled down to hermit life in earnest. He had tried the experiment of "Nature versus Medicine," and Nature had triumphed. With good health, with strange birds and flowers to study and identify, Walton decided he was content to spend a portion of his "rescued life" in Nature's company.

When younger, Walton had caught and caged many small animals such as deer mice, woodchucks, flying squirrels, stouts, mink and red and gray squirrels. His first captive in the cabin area was an artful old coon Walton named Satan. He was caught in a steel trap, the jaws of which had been wound with cloth to protect the animal's foot.

Satan's den was under a boulder near the cabin. Walton set the trap at the mouth of the den and covered it with leaves.

The next morning the trap, with clog attached, was missing, but Walton easily followed the raccoon's trail in the dead leaves. All the time he was in plain sight of the coon, who remained quiet until he realized that he was discovered, then made frantic efforts to escape. The clog, however, had anchored him securely to some witch hazel shrubs. The animal was full of fight, and Walton had to look out for his wicked teeth and vicious claws. The hermit brought along a stout piece of canvas, which he wrapped around the raccoon, trap and all, thus securing the animal's teeth and claws. Then he carried the raccoon to the cabin.

It took Walton two hours to get a strap on the raccoon's neck. The struggle was a desperate one, and without the canvas it would have been a victory for the raccoon. With the strap securely fastened and a dog chain attached, the trap was removed from the animal's foot and he was staked out near the cabin. For two weeks he tried night and day to free himself from collar and chain, then suddenly appeared contented.

As Walton says, "Instinct plays no part in coon lore. A coon can reason as well as the average human being. My captive proved to be as artful and wicked as Beelzebub himself."

Whenever unwatched, Satan would be up to all sorts of mischief. When caught red-handed, he would put on a look of innocence that made his master laugh. By the end of the first month he had learned about the hermit's way of life. If Walton went into the woods with his gun, on his return Satan would tear around in his cage, anxious for the squirrel he had not seen but was sure to get. When Walton went away without the gun, the raccoon paid no attention to his return. In this the animal was not guided by scent, for sometimes the wind would not be right. Without doubt he connected the gun and the squirrel in his mind, and perhaps he knew more about a gun than the hermit realized.

Satan did not take kindly to confinement, although his cage was under a small pine tree. When Walton was at the cabin he chained Satan to a tree and let him run outside. However, the hermit put him into the cage every day before going to the city for his mail. The raccoon resented this and would run up the pine tree when he saw his master lock the cabin door. One day Walton pulled him down and whipped him while the animal lay prone on the ground, his eyes covered. The hermit also took away his food and water. The raccoon never forgot the lesson. After that, whenever he saw Walton lock up, he would sneak into his cage, fearful that if found outside he would be whipped and starved. According to Walton, Satan preferred food in the following order: insects, eggs, birds or poultry, frogs, nuts, red squirrel, rabbit, gray squirrel and fish. This undoubtedly was the bill of fare of his wild state. He would not touch green corn or milk until Walton had crushed the former into his mouth and had dipped his nose into the latter. After this introduction, Satan would leave everything for the taste of milk.

One morning Hermit Walton opened up his cabin door to discover that a winter storm had left at least two inches of snow. A veritable mass of fox tracks surrounded a choice piece of meat he had nailed just too high to the trunk of a large pine tree. The tracks led away from the tree in an unusual trail: only three feet. Walton had seen these particular tracks before, for the animal who made them was no stranger to the area. Months before the hermit had appropriately named the fox Triplefoot.

After a short breakfast the hermit started on Triplefoot's trail. He followed the tracks all the way to a location where there were two ruined cellars and an ancient cultivated orchard. Triplefoot evidently had been foraging under some barberry bushes, for a drop or two of blood indicated she had caught and eaten a field mouse.

At that moment, far in the distance, the sound of two hounds could be heard in the area known as Solomon's Orchard. From their tone Walton knew that they were hot on the trail of the fox. Triplefoot's tracks now led the hermit across Magnolia Avenue, below the lily pond, along the ridges to

Mount Ann and then down to Coffin's Beach. There the sand dunes and the melted snow caused him to lose the trail. He noticed that the hounds also had been baffled at that point.

Hermit Walton realized that he probably should give up the effort, for there was not a track in sight in the shifting white sand or skirt of the woods near where Triplefoot's trail had left the beach. But he decided to backtrack toward the fox's den. Within ten minutes he located the trail again and found that the fox had crossed Magnolia Swamp south of Solomon's Orchard, then followed the ridges to the old quarry area.

Triplefoot's den was actually less than an eight-minute walk from the hermit's cabin. It was dark when Walton first located the den, and it reminded him for all the world of the den the great general Israel Putnam had entered when he pulled out the legendary wolf at extreme danger to his own life.*

One season Triplefoot reared a family. In April she stored two hens and a grouse in the den so that she would not have to hunt when her cubs were born. Later, when the cubs came out to play, the hermit spent hours watching them with a telescope. Once one of the three cubs suddenly appeared, saw Walton and coolly looked him over. Then he vanished, only to appear a moment later with another cub. Not over six feet away, they appeared fat and stocky "as two young pigs."

That fall Triplefoot's cubs were killed by hunters, leaving her childless. Her mate probably had been shot as well, for she did not rear a family the next year.

One item always puzzled Walton: the fact that Triplefoot did not go after poultry every day. Walton finally decided the fox reasoned that a wholesale slaughter of fowl would attract attention, and the irate farmers might make it a business to hunt for the fox den.

Walton and Triplefoot often met while tramping in the woods, and the fox soon understood that the hermit did not covet her glossy pelt. She frequently led pursuing hounds

* I cover the episode in my *Legends* volume, page 93.

through his cabin yard, always fooling them completely. Nevertheless, the hounds had a good scent, and matters finally became dangerous.

The end of Triplefoot's career came when a group of hounds evidently united in the chase after her, bringing her within reach of the gun of a hunter often seen by Hermit Walton. Triplefoot was hit by a bullet near Magnolia Swamp. Walton followed her into the swamp, where he found her under a boulder slowly dying from her wound and from exhaustion. Walton buried the body of his friend, glad that her beautiful robe and her mutilated body would not be separated in death.

Without question, Mason A. Walton, author of many articles in the famous *Youth's Companion, Forest and Stream* and the delightful 304-page book *A Hermit's Wild Friends,* was a great woodsman. During his eighteen years of real "hermiting," he put on paper many discoveries that should not be forgotten. He made for himself a permanent place among the world's outstanding naturalists.

3

Tragedy
of the *Eastland*

At a few minutes before 7:30 A.M. on the fateful morning of Saturday, July 24, 1915, the excursion steamer *Eastland,* with more than 2000 men, women and children aboard, overturned while tied to the dock at Clark and South Water streets in Chicago. Within minutes 812 people were dead; 23 more died of their injuries shortly afterward. Twenty-two families were totally wiped out. It was the worst disaster in terms of loss of life in Great Lakes history.

It had all begun as a festive occasion, the fifth annual picnic and excursion boat trip to Michigan City, Indiana, for employees of the Western Electric Company. It was sponsored by the Hawthorne Club, an educational and recreational organization for the workers. A contract had been signed between the chairman of the picnic committee, Charles J. Malmros, and the Indiana Transportation Company for five lake passenger steamers to accommodate the expected crowd.

The club indeed intended to have a crowd, for the contract provided for a substantial rebate to the organization on a sliding scale, the amount of rebate rising with the number of tickets sold at seventy-five cents each. With 9000 employees as potential purchasers, the club was in a position to add a great deal of money to its treasury, and efforts to sell tickets were more than enthusiastic. In fact, after the disaster more than one tale was told of coercion to buy tickets under threat of job loss. Peter Frisina, after identifying the body of his nineteen-year-old wife, cried out, "Oh, if I hadn't taken tickets, even if it cost me my job!" The father of drowned Agnes Kasperski later stated, "Agnes's fear of the water had been conquered by her fear of losing her job."

Many others, of course, were eagerly looking forward to the outing. Thus on the morning of July 24 thousands of families from Chicago and the suburbs of Cicero and Hawthorne were heading to the Chicago River near the Clark Street bridge, where the five steamers were moored. Departure times were staggered as follows: *Eastland,* 7:30 A.M.; *Theodore Roosevelt,* 8 A.M.; *Petoskey,* 8:30 A.M.; *Racine,* 10 A.M.; and *Rochester,* 2:30 P.M.

The *Eastland* * was the craft on which most of the excursionists wished to travel, for it was claimed she had a speed of over thirty miles an hour, making her the fastest ship on the lakes. A trip on the *Eastland,* leaving the earliest and going the fastest, meant the longest time at the picnic—or so those who boarded her thought.

Not one of the excited crowd knew that sailors on the Great Lakes were calling the *Eastland* a "cranky ship." On several occasions her instability had been demonstrated when she listed badly to port. On July 17, 1904, with 2142 passengers sailing from South Haven to Chicago, those aboard were ordered to shift to the starboard side to correct her imbalance. For some reason, perhaps fear, they refused to move until the fire hose was turned on them. This method proved effective.

---

* As furnished by the *United States Shipping List of Merchants for 1906,* the *Eastland* had the official number 200031 and was steamship-rigged. She had been built in 1903 at Port Huron, Michigan, with a horsepower of 3000. Gross tonnage was 1961, with a net tonnage of 1218. Her length was 265 feet; breadth, 38.2; depth 19.5. Her crew numbered seventy four plus the captain. The *Eastland,* with Chicago as her home port, was in service to carry passengers.

Ignorant of these facts, Western Electric employees happily jostled each other in their efforts to get on board the doomed ship.

A short time before seven o'clock several of the earliest arrivals noticed a slight list to port. Observing this list himself, Chief Engineer Joseph M. Erickson decided to open the starboard ballast tank and seacock. Unfortunately not only was the list corrected, but soon the vessel began a list toward starboard. Helping Erickson at this time was John Elbert, a survivor of the *Titanic*. The listing condition continued, changing several times from side to side. At 7:16 there was a slight list to port; two minutes later the *Eastland* heeled in the opposite direction, then listed slightly to port again; at 7:23 she listed sharply to port. Erickson now sent men to the main deck to tell the passengers to go to starboard, but only a few obeyed.

Captain Harry Pedersen was alarmed. Realizing the potential for disaster because of the listing, he shouted down from the starboard bridge to open the inside doors and let the people back onto the pier. Unfortunately he was a few seconds too late, for the *Eastland* began her ominous fatal swing to port. Tons of water poured through the open ports and gangway doors. A weird mass of popcorn machines, candy boxes, entire refreshment stands, picnic baskets, crushed and leaking lemonade barrels, ship bulkheads and furniture, together with men, women and children, slid into the portside pilings as the *Eastland* rolled over on her side on the bottom of the river. Less than eight feet of her starboard side remained above water, giving the *Eastland* the look of a massive whale.

One man who survived, Theodore Soderstrom, later described the scene on board the *Eastland* at the terrible moment the vessel went over: "The passengers were crowded on the outer rail from ten to thirty deep in places. I noticed the boat beginning to career slightly, but at first it gave me no uneasiness. Then just before we pulled out, several hundred passengers who had been saying good-bye to persons on the dock came over to the outer [port] rail. Almost instantly the boat lurched drunkenly, righted itself, then pitched once more.

"By this time passengers knew there was something wrong. But it all happened so quickly that no one knew just what to do. For a third time the boat lurched, this time slowly, and there were screams as everyone tried to get to the side of the vessel next to the dock. Many were beaten down to the deck unconscious in this mad rush. Probably a dozen persons—it might have been more—jumped into the water. But they were crushed under the side of the boat before they had a chance to swim away, for after the boat got part way over, it seemed to drop on its side like a stone."

Traveling over the Clark Street bridge on his way home from market, Mike Javanco, his wagon loaded with vegetables, could not believe what he saw. Knowing nothing about ships, he instinctively realized something was terribly wrong. Leaning far over the bridge, he called to the crowd of young men on the bow to get off the boat. They jeered at his accent, and chose death. Javanco jumped from his wagon, ran across the bridge and soon was on the dock helping to rescue scores of passengers.

A few hundred people, most of them from the upper deck, managed to climb over the starboard rail to find relative safety on the exposed side of the craft. But the water around the steamer was teeming with men, women and children desperately struggling for their lives.

Seeing what was happening, the lineman on the tug *Kenosha* had cut the towline between the two craft. The tug's captain realized that the powerful propeller of his craft would cause terrible injury to the hundreds of people thrashing in the water. He backed the *Kenosha* against the now horizontal bow of the *Eastland*, forming a bridge by which many of the passengers reached shore.

After the initial shock of seeing the *Eastland* roll over, witnesses on shore quickly began throwing all available objects that would float into the water. Every craft on the river raced to the scene. Passengers on the *Theodore Roosevelt* threw the lifesavers from their vessel to the people in the water.

N. W. LeVally, manager of the Oxweld Acetylene Company, rushed his men to the exposed side of the *Eastland,* where they could hear the cries of trapped passengers who were hammering for release from what had become an underwater prison. To the amazement of torchman J. H. Rista, he was ordered by Captain Pedersen to stop his work of cutting an escape hole. Rista refused to obey him, and eventually forty people were pulled from certain death through that very hole. A few more passengers were taken out alive through other holes torched in the hull.

Not a single member of the crew was lost, many of them having clambered over the rail and jumped to the dock before the final list. But for 835 passengers, this was their last excursion.

Free funeral service was provided for families left destitute, and plans were completed for community funeral services in the various churches of Cicero and neighboring suburbs. So many funeral processions passed through the streets of Cicero on the Wednesday following the disaster that the day has since been known as Black Wednesday.

Victor A. Olander, secretary of the Lake Seamen's Union, aroused governmental and public outrage with his statement that many other ships on the lakes were as dangerous as the *Eastland* because of faulty construction. He held that the *Eastland* was not properly designed, and that the water ballast system was not the main fault. He charged that United States inspectors under Captain Charles H. Westcott of Detroit, chief of the lake district, had played into the hands of ship owners at the expense of sailors and passengers. He said this was shown by the fact that thirty-one ships, passed by the inspectors, had sunk in the Great Lakes since 1905, several of them taking all on board to their deaths.

The announcement by detectives from the State Attorney's office that they had seized tickets taken from the passengers boarding the *Eastland* further increased public outrage. They asserted that these tickets numbered 2550 and did not account for children, musicians and the seventy-two crew members. They estimated that the total number of persons aboard the steamer might have been 2800 or more. The lessees of the ship asserted that 2408 passenger tickets had been collected.

According to records, the temporary inspection certificate issued June 4, 1913, by U.S. inspectors at Cleveland allowed the *Eastland* to carry 2000 passengers. A later temporary certification, dated June 15, 1915, permitted the craft to carry 2253. But a third certificate, issued only twenty-two days before the disaster, granted permission for the *Eastland* to carry 2570 passengers.

State Attorney Hoyne seized correspondence between officers of the Hawthorne Club and the Indiana Transportation Company, and the issue of overcrowding the boat was added to a growing list of questions about the disaster. Hoyne declared that Captain Pedersen of the *Eastland* told him that federal sanction for increasing the carrying capacity without change in construction was "arranged," and that Pedersen was told to go to Grand Haven, Michigan, and get the certificate.

When actual rescue operations had ceased and the dead were still being identified, the coroner's jury was assembled to find out what had happened and how. The inquiry, under Cook County Coroner Peter Hoffman, took six full days.*

Victim Kate Austin was chosen as typical of the 835 who perished as a result of the *Eastland* disaster. The evidence given applied to all lives lost.

The inquest began on Tuesday, July 24, 1915, in Room 811 of the County Building in Chicago. Starting the proceedings, the coroner spoke slowly and clearly:

"Gentlemen, I shall ask you to keep as quiet as possible during the hearing and during this investigation, in order that

---

* The *Transcript of Testimony* of Coroner Hoffman's investigation, an impressive booklet of 156 pages, is available today at the Boston Athenaeum.

the jurors and all interested may hear the evidence given here.
I shall ask the Chief of Police and the Sheriff to keep absolute
order. I don't want anybody around the aisles unless they can
be seated, and unless they are absolutely interested they will
have to leave the room, outside of the Police and Sheriff. It is
hot in this room and close, and absolute order will be necessary so the jurors may hear the testimony."

The coroner went on to explain that the State of Illinois was
represented by Mr. Hoyne and Mr. Sullivan, plus several assis-
tants. He also explained that the State Attorney was cooperat-
ing with the coroner, and that it was his privilege to question
the witnesses "because I may not be able to bring out the full
facts."

Congressman A. J. Sabath now told the coroner that "at
a meeting of Bohemian-American citizens of the City of
Chicago, a nationality which has suffered a great deal in this
disaster, I have been requested by the General Committee to
represent it in any way possible."

The first witness was R. J. Moore, a passenger on the *Eastland*. When he arrived at the *Eastland* at about seven o'clock
that July morning and started down the stairs to board the
boat, "there was a long line, five or six abreast." His testimony
continued as follows: "As I was going along the side of the
boat, I saw water coming out of there; I saw it by the ton—I
remarked to a gentleman, they were taking out a lot of ballast;
he said, 'It isn't ballast, it is exhaust steam.'

"I thought it was throwing out a lot of steam. It was about
7:10, and the first indication of the boat listing was about eight
or nine minutes before it went down, when the refrigerator in
the bar was thrown over with all the bottles and made a terrific
crash. I was on the second floor and could see the bottles on
the floor from that end. The boat started to list north, and if
they were given a signal at that time, I think most of the people
could have gotten off the boat.

"From that time on, the boat kept listing. I tried to get on the
south side; there were a little batch of ladies and children, and

I took a chance and went with the crowd. I went through the staircase, and just as I struck the floor, the water struck me. I got up in some part of the boat and worked my way through—I suppose about the width of this umbrella and maybe fourteen feet long; it was filled with women and children. They were all saved. I don't know if any of them are here or not.

"I was pulled out second to last by one of the firemen. I think he belonged to a tugboat. I hung on down in there for thirty-five minutes before I was taken out. When I came out, I wandered away; my clothes were all torn and I was dazed."

The question was now asked how long it was from the time the boat began to list to the port, or north side, up to the time it toppled over. Mr. Moore answered that it was from eight to ten minutes, and the boat was "going all the time." Mr. Moore was asked to estimate how many people were on the upper deck; he answered "about 800 or 900 people." When asked about children on board, he stated that there were "a lot of boys and girls there from the age of eight up to fifteen, running around, having a good time, trying to locate themselves," and he agreed with the coroner that there were many children below the age of five.

Another witness was Algernon Richey, a solicitor. At the time of the disaster he stood with the bridge tender of the railroad company at the north end of the Clark Street bridge from seven o'clock until she went over. "I saw her start to list. We commented upon it in every way, commented upon it until it got to the top of the middle deck doors. She got to the top of that and commenced to list more, fast, and the crowd on the boat deck, the hurricane deck, started to the south; they ran to the south rail, starboard side. They ran over and it seemed their feet—probably the boat went faster; she went down quick after that. It seemed as if she were overbalanced at the time.

"The bridge tender and I ran down on the pier on the bridge. We threw in everything we could find that was loose. We went down on the dock on the south side of the river; the ship chandlers there threw out coil after coil of rope. We made them fast and threw them into the river, and pulled out three, four and five at a time. I am a good swimmer myself, even with one hand, but I didn't dare go into the water."

Adam F. Weckler was harbor master of Chicago. His duties included wharves, bridges, moving of vessels and everything to do with the harbor and river. He had arrived at the Clark Street bridge at 7:10. According to Weckler's testimony, "The boat at that time was listed to port, just coming over, about a five- to six-degree list. I stood down on the dock and called to Captain Pedersen on the bridge, and I asked him to put in his water ballast and trim her up. He said he was trimming all the time. In the meantime he had given the 'stand-by' order and cast off the stern line. The dockman ran forward to see what line he wanted thrown off. I would not let him throw off the line. I told Captain Pedersen to trim her up. He held up his hand to state that he was trimming as fast as he could. He stepped out to the outside of the bridge. The boat kept turning, and he shouted to the people to get off the best way they could, and the boat, I should say, around in eight or ten minutes' time, laid right on the side."

Weckler was asked for his opinion, as a harbor master with seventeen years' experience in navigation and boat building, what he believed caused the boat to go over. He responded, "I don't think there was any water in their tanks, to start with."

Congressman Sabath then asked him, "Is it your opinion, if the Government limited the capacity of the boat to 1200 instead of 2500, that the accident would not have happened under the circumstances that it happened?"

Weckler answered, "Well, I do not think it would."

Harbor Master Weckler was then asked how he knew that the *Eastland* did not carry water. He replied, "On account of the way she trimmed, she is always lunging on the side, she is never ready until the moment she ships off, she always gives a lunge according to the side she is tied, but I know the boat so well, I never was much—I know she doesn't carry water, that is why I have been trying to find out why she did not carry water, the only satisfaction that I ever got was they did not need any water."

Joseph R. Lynn, assistant harbor master, stated that on the day of the accident when he was at the *Eastland*'s midship gangway, "it appeared to me she had considerable of a side list, more so than I had seen her have at any other time that I have been down to the dock at the Rush Street bridge.

"The list was to the out, the port, and the starboard means the river side, and I walked along there to where her spring line was, and met Mr. Weckler, the harbor master, and I made the remark, 'Ad, she has got quite a list,' and he says, 'Yes, it is a shame to let that boat go out with that load on her.' And I looked down the bridge at the same time, about, and saw Captain Pedersen there, and I says, 'Good morning, Captain,' and he answered me back, and Captain Weckler said, 'Are you taking in your water ballast?' He nodded and said, 'Yes, I am trimming,' and he left the starboard side of the boat and walked out of our sight. I noticed that the spring line was particularly tight, and I tested it with my foot; and I walked to her waist line. It wasn't in line forward, and I noticed that it had a considerable of a side list. I went forward to the head line, and it didn't seem long, and came back again. I think that I had walked over the after gangway the third time, and back to the spring line again, and she had gone over four inches to my idea, what I had seen her former mark, for the water had gone down again, and I would say then she was very close to an eighteen-inch list, from observation. She was down; her bow was pretty near off the dock, and her stern was in close to the dock to take the passengers down there.

"I went forward again to where I could look across her stem, and I leaned against the building and looked up at her so that I would be perfectly firm, and wouldn't be swaying, and I saw her going. I hollered to Mr. Weckler, 'The boat is going over, get off. If she goes, we are going with her.' At that Mr. Weckler appeared by the stairway and I heard him holler, 'Ed!' I looked up and saw him coming out of the gangway, and my first impulse was to get back to a telephone, which I did.

"I ran up the stairs on the approach of the bridge, south to the iron bridge, and goes [sic] back to the City of South Haven dock, and, arriving on the first floor, I had to go west 150 feet, then back to get up another flight of stairs, and then came in here and got into the South Haven steamboat line's office. I got a telephone and immediately telephoned the City Hall and had them send all the ambulances and pulmotors and lung motors, and to notify the police department and the fire department that the *Eastland* was turned over.

"That is an interval of nine or ten minutes from the time I landed on that dock, and I set the telephone down and looked out, and saw that the tug was in close under her bow, and that they were jumping onto that, and the people were climbing over her side—the starboard side—in over the side, and some were jumping out into the river, and throwing life preservers and other things, and the dockmen were throwing everything. I grabbed a telephone book, hunting for the city boat company, to come and cut holes in her—upon her—between what you would call her second, you would call that the second main deck—that is, her cabin deck. An opportunity to get out would have to be through those portholes—those on the starboard side were going over the rail to get on her side and stand on them, and I tried to look at it, and I didn't know where to look for it, for those ox-welders, because they had to cut places for them in order to get down into the cabin. I tried the big phone—the regular day company's phone. . . . I was unable to get this tug company on the phone."

John H. O'Meara of the tug *Kenosha* was dispatched to help the steamer *Eastland* at 6:55. "When I got there I tied up to a cluster of piles just south of the abutment on the south side of the bridge. I put a line over and let the tug drift, drift so she would lay out of the way of all water craft passing back and forth there.

"I went up in the pilot house and sat down there and the tug laid in this position with a slack line, and I should judge about 7:25 or so—maybe not that late—someone hollered on the deck, 'All ready, Captain,' and something about a bridge.

"Then I lay there without the engine working waiting for the 'All right' signal from the captain. After a considerable length of time, I couldn't say how much—I should judge five to seven minutes—I began to get uneasy. The signal wasn't coming; the captain didn't work his stern out. . . . The boat listed slowly to port and she hesitated. I didn't think there was anything wrong at the time. I began to notice the boat more closely and she began to list more gradually. She kind of hesitated and kind of seemed to stay there; I couldn't say how long, and I heard someone say something—I don't know whether it was the captain or not. Then there was a roar and a scream and screeching of people and over it went."

The controversy and litigation involving the *Eastland* went on for twenty years. Finally, on August 7, 1935, the decision was handed down that the owners of the *Eastland* were not to blame. The Court held that the boat was seaworthy, that the operators had taken proper precautions and that the responsibility was traced to an engineer who neglected to fill the ballast tanks properly.

Thus ended the story of the *Eastland* disaster, a catastrophe that claimed 835 lives—585 more than were lost in the Chicago Fire. This tragedy has always interested me strangely because to those who perished "the sea" was only a romantic dream, far away and unknown. Yet they met their deaths in a watery grave as final as any the ocean has ever opened to the unsuspecting.

4

The Disaster-Prone
Circassian

As I walked along the New York State beach from Shinnecock Light, Long Island, on September 11, 1937, toward the last resting place of the iron ship *Circassian,* I thought how she had been hounded by disaster time and time again.

This 280-foot vessel was originally built as a steamer in England, the country whose flag she flew. At the time of the Civil War she was captured under humiliating circumstances while running the blockade for the South. The Fulton ferryboat *Somerset,* with her double ends, had been remodeled and fitted with heavy guns by the United States.* Encountering the *Circassian* off the coast of Cuba, the *Somerset* ordered her to come about. Inclined at first to disregard this order from a renovated ferryboat, the captain of the *Circassian* hastily changed his mind when a few shots impressed him with the caliber of the guns mounted on the *Somerset*'s deck. The *Circassian* hove to at once and surrendered, yielding to her captors a rich haul of badly needed goods valued at $315,371.29.

After the war the *Circassian* was purchased by shipping

---

* Because the *Somerset* had been built to withstand the hard knocks of ferry service, it was believed she would make an effective gunboat.

interests, only to be wrecked a short time later at lonely Sable Island. The famous New York wrecker, Captain John Lewis of the Columbian Wrecking Company, succeeded in pulling her off the treacherous sands on which she had grounded.

Sailing later for New York, the *Circassian* went ashore again at Squam, New Jersey, in December 1869. Refloated once more, she was put in drydock. During most of the next three years she was repaired and made over into a sailing vessel. Finally the proud *Circassian* was seaworthy again and set out under a full spread of sails.

In November 1876 she was making a return voyage from Liverpool to New York with a crew of thirty-seven. A week after sailing down the Mersey River, she sighted a dismasted wreck at sea. Captain Richard Williams ordered a boat put over, and twelve survivors were taken from the waterlogged craft.

Unknown to the captain at this time, there was a substantial error in his ship's compass. On December 11, while approaching the American coast, the *Circassian* ran into a heavy snowstorm. Around midnight, with visibility reduced to a few yards, she entered an area of heavy seas where the sound of breaking waves was plainly heard. Before her course could be changed, the great ship ran upon a bar one quarter mile from land, near the Shinnecock Life Saving Station on Long Island, New York.

Although the *Circassian* was sighted at once, it was impossible for Captain Baldwin Cook of the Life Saving Station to launch a lifeboat because of the mountainous combers that the northeast gale was sending toward the beach. At the same time the ship's great draught of almost twenty feet prevented these breakers from working her in toward shore over the bar.

She was too far out to be reached by breeches buoy, for the shot line would never have crossed the four hundred yards to the ship against the teeth of the gale. Even if it had, there was no assurance that the survivors could find the line in the blackness of night. Therefore the lifesavers could do nothing but wait for dawn, when the tide would go down and the apparatus could be set up much closer to the vessel.

Lifesavers from the two nearby stations, Numbers 9 and 11, were on the scene when dawn broke. All hands pitched in to make ready the first shot. Whistling through the air, the projectile fell short. Again the gun was loaded; again failure resulted. Finally, on the third try, the weight fell squarely on the deck of the *Circassian*. The sailors quickly made the line secure. All was put in readiness to send out the lifecar, but at low water the storm relented and the waves subsided so rapidly that the lifecar was no longer necessary.

The surfboat was promptly launched. In seven trips all forty-nine shipwrecked sailors and passengers were taken safely ashore. After being shipwrecked twice on one crossing of the Atlantic, they finally felt firm ground under them. After arrangements had been made, they dispatched with gratitude to New York City.

Still the old *Circassian* was not finished. Although every one had been landed safely, wreckers in the vicinity believed there was a good chance of salvaging the rebuilt iron ship that already had so much unusual history.

The Coast Wrecking Company of New York sent its representatives down to Long Island to save the unlucky vessel. Captain Perrin cooperated with the local agent, Captain Charles A. Pierson of Bridgehampton. Captain John Lewis, who had pulled the ship from the sands of Sable Island, was given the task of doing his work again under more difficult circumstances.

As soon as the gale subsided, Captain Lewis started salvage operations. He hired three engineers from New York, ten members of a nearby Shinnecock Indian tribe and two other local men. In addition, sixteen of the original crew returned to the *Circassian* and were ready to hoist sail and take her away from the dangerous sands once she was afloat.

The ship had been swung around broadside to the waves by the storm. Most of her weight was supported amidships, with her bow and stern under constant strain. Heavy anchors were sunk far to seaward and immense hawsers ran between the anchors and ship, with continuous tension being kept on these lines. It was hoped that eventually the combined forces of high tide, hawsers and heavy ocean swells would lift the *Circassian* and gradually pull her out of the sand. Within fourteen days she had actually moved 295 feet; at dead low water she rested 308 yards from the beach.

It is easy to say what should have been done after a disaster has occurred. Hindsight indicates that a line ought to have been stretched from ship to shore as a precaution for those who were gambling their lives in order to free this vessel. The *Circassian* required a brisk northeasterly gale so she could be taken out to sea. Unfortunately, as every lifesaver knew, such a wind might well develop into a bad storm, and the ship would then be in exactly the same trouble as when she was originally stranded. The wrecking company decided that no line should be stretched between the ship and the shore because they anticipated that once the wind developed, the Shinnecock Indians, as well as the sailors, would use it to flee prematurely to safety. The *Circassian* would then never get off the beach. To be fair to the wreckers, they also felt that the great iron ship would never break up and that the thirty-two men living aboard her were perfectly safe.

The storm they awaited began to develop on December 26, a good northeasterly blow with threatening weather. The winds increased daily until, by December 29, the lighters that had been alongside removing cargo fled for shelter. The last cargo gang, led by Captain Luther D. Burnett, came ashore at ten o'clock that morning. From then on there was no communication with the *Circassian*.

People gathered up and down the shore to watch the so-called second launching of the ship. Everyone believed she would float at high water and go to sea under canvas. But by noon the wind developed into a gale, and snow mixed with biting sleet began to sweep the vicinity. By four o'clock in the afternoon tremendous seas were crashing against the hulk of the *Circassian*, which began to roll and pound heavily on the bar. Probably her iron hull was already beginning to break.

Then onlookers watching from shore noticed that her great hawsers were being slackened. It appeared as if those on board realized the futility of attempting to free her from the bar and were giving the waves a chance to push the *Circassian* nearer to the beach, where they might be rescued. Until this time there had been no sign from the *Circassian* that anyone aboard was trying to get to shore.

Around seven o'clock distress signals went out from the stricken craft, but it was too late to try to send a boat for the men. Crews from Life Saving Stations 9, 10 and 11 were called; Captain Baldwin Cook made initial preparations for rescuing men from the luckless *Circassian* for the second time within eighteen days.

The ocean beach sidesaddling the ship presented a strange spectacle that night. The sea had come up across the higher part of the shore, sweeping in around the hummocks and sand dunes, even reaching out for the distant beach hills and pouring through their sluiceways. Because of this, Captain Cook was forced to retreat seventy-two yards farther back, almost to the shelter of the dunes.

A hurricane was now blowing. Giant billows cascaded across the decks of the *Circassian,* and every sailor was perched high in the rigging. No lifeboat could maneuver in the awesome cross-sea that enveloped the *Circassian* from all points, creating a veritable caldron of foam and water.

The ocean flooded the beach still higher. The combination of surf and wind, rain and sleet, freezing cold and a hail of wet sand became almost unbearable for the lifesavers. Then they found they had to change their location in order to reposition the shot-line gun. A change in wind direction necessitated moving westward of the stranded ship, which took considerable time. Trouble next developed in getting match rope to burn.

Finally the gun was ready to fire. Three times the shot left the gun, described its parabola in the sky and fell short of its goal. Each time the long lines were hauled back and made ready again. At last it became apparent that no shot could reach the *Circassian*—even if it did, it would be physically impossible for the survivors to use the line.

Around midnight the tide began to go out. Lights were observed on deck, indicating that the hull still held together, but the wreck must have been cleared of everything by the fearful sea. At two in the morning survivors who had been in the foremast were seen taking refuge in the mizzen rigging.

Ninety minutes later the *Circassian* snapped completely in two. Her forepart settled down outside the bar, while her stern beat across the shoal closer to shore.

Still the iron mizzenmast stood erect, the rigging crowded with men whose shouts of despair could be heard even above the roar of wind and waves. A short time later the tall spar began to dip and swing as it worked loose from its supports. The frantic lifesavers could only watch the gyrations of that mast crowded with anguished humanity, realizing that they were about to witness one of the great tragedies of the sea.

Back and forth the great pole swung, until finally it bent far over to port with its heavy load. Beyond recovery, it gradually lowered and began to submerge in the giant seas. One by one the men were pulled away and washed toward shore, drowning in the breakers. Those who remained in the rigging perished alongside the ship as the mast settled under water.

Superintendent H. E. Huntington, in charge of all lifesaving stations on Long Island, organized a lantern squad of twenty men to search for bodies or possible survivors, although there was little hope that anyone could get to shore alive. The current ran with great force in an easterly direction outside the breakers, which made the chance of reaching shore extremely remote.

Suddenly, however, a group of lifesavers noticed a strange weaving mass caught in a huge breaker just about to crash on the beach. What they actually saw was a large cylindrical piece of cork, five feet long and eleven inches in diameter, fitted with straps and beckets for use in salvage work. The first and second mates had noticed the object aboard the *Circassian* and had grabbed it when they were about to be washed overboard. They were submerged in the cross-sea for a time, but then the buoyancy of the cork brought them to the surface. The ship's carpenter and one of the seamen hired by the wreckers quickly grabbed onto the floating buoy.

The first mate realized that four men could swamp the cork and cause everyone to drown unless they were careful. "Lock your legs together with mine and with each other!" he shouted in a voice of authority above the roar of the storm. They obeyed at once, thus stabilizing the rocking buoy and maintaining a safe equilibrium with each other. They were now a single mass of buoy and humanity, battered by the waves but slowly being pushed away from the ship. Watching the action of the sea, the chief mate ordered the men to begin kicking slowly toward the shore as they clung onto their handholds. Despite the reverse action of the easterly sweep, they made slow progress toward the shore.

Just before a wave swept over them, the mate would give the order to hold their breath. By the time the surf had passed, they would be able to refill their lungs with air. Then came the moment when they were sighted at the crest of a breaking wave.

On the beach a great shout went up when the buoy was seen. A human chain rushed into the water to meet the great breaking billow head-on as it collapsed and swept up the shore.

Kicking hard every moment against the dangerous undertow, the men rode the buoy until they were only waist-deep in water. As the wave paused momentarily before receding, the lifesavers reached them. Soon the entire mass of twirling buoy and shouting men was slowly making progress toward the beach.

Finally the men and the buoy were beyond reach of the next wave. The four survivors were carried to the nearest guard station, where they were put to bed at once. Because of the cleverness and bravery of the first mate, four men had been saved from almost certain death. But they were the only ones rescued of the thirty-two aboard ship at the start of the gale. The *Circassian* had ended her career.

Part Six

1940–Present

1

Spies from U-Boat Landings

Shortly after dawn on Saturday, June 13, 1942, four German saboteurs disembarked on the American shore. They landed unopposed at Amagansett on Long Island, barely one hundred miles from New York City.

Jeanette Rattray, gifted author from nearby East Hampton, writes in *Ship Ashore!* that within twenty-four hours of the arrival of the spies, the entire East Hampton township was alerted. However, many people did not take the landing seriously until FBI Director J. Edgar Hoover announced it was a fact weeks later.

Not only did German U-boats send ashore those four saboteurs, they also landed four more at Ponte Vedra Beach in Florida. In both cases the men had come ashore in collapsible rubber boats with substantial sums of money, clothing and explosives, which they buried at once above the waterline. They had a complete two-year plan of destruction aimed at American industries and utilities.

On the evening of June 12, 1942, "Den Mother" Mrs. Jeanette Rattray took her Cub Scouts for a late afternoon picnic at East Hampton. One of the Scouts down on the beach

183

heard the sound of a Diesel engine. He wondered why, for he knew no beam trawler would venture inside the bar just offshore. The entire group went to the shore to look out over the water. They could see nothing because of the breakers and the foggy weather.

Later, around eight o'clock that night, a summer resident drawing blackout curtains heard the sound of an engine where the saboteurs actually landed. A Coastguardsman patrolling the area stopped by and told her it was probably one of the new Navy patrol craft. At about this time Lothar-Gunther Buchheim * was in the general area aboard a submarine.

Shortly after midnight on June 14, Surfman 2nd Class James Cullen of the Coast Guard began his six-mile patrol along the beach from the Amagansett station. When he had walked a relatively short distance, a stranger dressed in civilian clothes came up the beach out of the fog. A short distance away two men in bathing trunks were wading out of the water, followed by a fourth man carrying and dragging what he told the Coastguardsman was a bag full of clams.

Cullen was not convinced and continued to question them. The "civilian" then got tough. He told Cullen they would not kill him if the Coastguardsman could "keep his mouth shut"; $260 was offered as bribe money.

"Would you know me if you saw me again?" asked the saboteur.

Cullen answered in the negative. The two men then parted.

Cullen went back to his station at Amagansett, breaking into a run as soon as he had covered enough distance so that the Germans could not see him. At the station he turned over the bribe money to the man in charge, Carl Jenette. Immediately the station was electrified with activity. Jenette telephoned Warrant Officer Oden and Chief Boatswain's Mate Warren Barnes. They began a visual search of the ocean and before long actually saw the submarine through a rift in the fog,

* His book *U-Boat War* cannot be surpassed.

observing that the U-boat was on a course to the east.

Four members of the Coast Guard then took rifles and began intensive exploration of the area on foot. As soon as the Army and Navy were put on alert, soldiers joined in systematically searching the dunes. They discovered German cigarettes as well as a pair of wet bathing trunks. Freshly disturbed sand caught the attention of the searchers; they dug out four wooden, tin-lined cases of explosives. More German clothes and an overseas cap with a swastika then were unearthed.

The saboteurs had purchased four tickets to Jamaica, Long Island, at about 6:45 that morning from Station Agent Ira Baker at Amagansett. A search turned up clothing left by the saboteurs under a hedge near the station.

On June 20, 22, 23 and 27 the eight saboteurs who had landed from U-boats at Amagansett and at Ponte Vedra Beach were arrested. After their capture, two confessed. Six of the men were executed, the seventh was sentenced to thirty years in prison and the eighth received life imprisonment.

Following the U-boat landing at Amagansett, men of the Coast Guard carried rifles, revolvers and flashlights in addition to their standard Coston signals and regulation time clocks for the duration of the war. Before this they had been unarmed.

James Cullen of the Coast Guard was later promoted to coxswain and given a medal for his handling of the situation on June 14, 1942. In Washington, D.C., the FBI has an exhibit of mementos from the saboteurs' landing.

At least four U-boat landings along the Atlantic coast occurred during World War II. The one at Amagansett and the one in Florida, not far from Jacksonville, have been reported fully by Allen Hynd in *Passport to Treason* and by Colonel Vernon Hinchley in *Spy Mysteries Unveiled*.

A Cape Cod World War II landing from a U-boat was revealed to me by C. Graham Hurlburt, Jr., of Cohasset, Massachusetts. The landing was said to have been on Cape Cod's Dennis Beach between Lighthouse Inn and the entrance to

Bass River. German radio equipment was later found there.

The fourth U-boat incident took place on the coast of Maine in the town of Hancock. American-born William Colepaugh and German national Eric Gimpel came ashore there in a rubber raft from Nazi U-boat *1230*.

Actually, FBI records on one of the spies went back several years. William Curtis Colepaugh had been under observation for some time. In June 1940 an FBI special agent in Boston was informed that customs officers had observed Colepaugh from May 2 to May 27, 1940. During that time he visited the German tanker *Pauline Friederich*, which was tied up at Battery Wharf in Boston.

The customs official stated that Colepaugh claimed he was engaged as a painter aboard the vessel. While visiting the German tanker, he often spoke of going to Germany to study engineering. It was also reported that he expressed dissatisfaction with conditions in the United States and was interested in leaving this country.

It occurred to customs officials that because of Colepaugh's dissatisfaction the FBI might wish to conduct inquiries concerning him. Thus a case was opened on William Colepaugh. Instructions were issued to make necessary checks to determine whether he was engaged in subversive activities.

Investigation revealed that William, born March 25, 1918, had been a student of naval architecture and engineering at Massachusetts Institute of Technology. Records of this college show that he entered in September 1938 after attending secondary school in Toms River, New Jersey. His home address was listed as Niantic, Connecticut.

Because of scholastic difficulties, Colepaugh left MIT on February 6, 1941. The name of one of his former roommates was obtained. This young man advised investigators that Colepaugh often received mail containing propaganda publications from the German consul in Boston and also from German news agencies in New York. He indicated that Colepaugh showed more than ordinary interest in these publications.

Customs guards stationed at the wharf where the *Pauline Friederich* had been docked remembered Colepaugh. One guard indicated that Colepaugh claimed he was living on board. When asked if he was a crew member of that ship, he replied that he was not but lived on board because he liked the crew members.

Another customs guard said that he once stopped Colepaugh attempting to board the ship and asked what his business was on board the vessel. The suspect replied that he had permission from the chief officer to spend a few days aboard the *Pauline Friederich*. When questioned by the customs guard why he wanted to go on a German ship, Colepaugh answered that the persons on board were treating him well and that he liked them better than the people in the United States.

A retired customs guard remembered seeing Colepaugh in the company of the first officer of the *Pauline Friederich*. He said he also had seen him in the dining room with the captain of the ship. The FBI also learned that in August 1940 William Colepaugh had two German sailors from the *Pauline Friederich* as weekend guests at his home in Niantic, Connecticut. Colepaugh's current address was unknown. One individual advised that he might be in South America as a crewman aboard a merchant vessel.

It was not until fourteen months later that Colepaugh again attracted the attention of the FBI. One afternoon in August 1941 a young midshipman from the United States Naval Academy walked into the FBI field office in Washington, D.C., and reported that he had roomed with William Curtis Colepaugh at a secondary school in New Jersey from September 1937 to June 1938. He was anxious to let the FBI know about him. He said that he visited Colepaugh in March 1940 at MIT and was taken to the German tanker *Pauline Friederich*. It appeared to the midshipman that his former roommate was well acquainted with the officers on board that ship. As they were leaving the ship, Colepaugh stated he was in favor of Germany and that he wanted to go there on the *Pauline Friederich*.

The midshipman further related that in June 1940 Colepaugh visited him in Groton, Connecticut. During a discussion of the war, Colepaugh was asked where his affiliation would lie if the United States went to war against Germany. His reply was that his affiliation probably would be with Germany.

The midshipman stated that he never had an occasion to meet Colepaugh after this incident, but what had been said bothered him. He felt that Colepaugh's attitude toward Germany warranted investigation.

All this time the FBI was building up data concerning Colepaugh. They learned he had either sold or given a radio receiving set to a former attaché at the German consulate in Boston. Reportedly Colepaugh had built this set himself.

Information was also received that Colepaugh often dropped in at a German tavern frequented by members of the German consulate in Boston. On one occasion Colepaugh stated that he had just returned from England on a British freighter.

On July 23, 1942, the *Scania*, a Swedish vessel, arrived at Philadelphia from Buenos Aires. The crew list of that vessel indicated that William Colepaugh was aboard as a seaman. He was questioned by local naval officers, at which time he presented a draft card indicating he had registered under the provisions of the Selective Training and Service Act on October 16, 1940. During this interview he admitted that he had not communicated with his local draft board, explaining that he had never received any communications from that board. This information was immediately turned over to the government, and Colepaugh was interviewed by FBI agents.

A check of draft board records in Boston, where Colepaugh had registered, revealed he had failed to return a completed questionnaire and had also failed to keep the board advised of his address. These were violations of a federal law under the investigative jurisdiction of the FBI. Accordingly, FBI agents in Boston contacted the local United States attorney. On July 25, 1942, a complaint was filed against William C. Colepaugh, charging him with violating the Selective Training and Service Act. A warrant was issued for his arrest.

Colepaugh was returned to Boston, where he was interviewed by FBI agents. He said that he was born in East Lyme, Connecticut, and claimed that his father was a native-born American. His mother, however, was born aboard the German ship *The Havel* en route to the United States. The suspect explained that while he was a student at MIT he met the captain of the German tanker *Pauline Friederich* and was invited to visit the ship. He did so on several occasions, becoming acquainted with a man he knew to be a Nazi party leader on board the vessel. On two occasions Colepaugh took this party leader home as a guest.

Colepaugh said that he had purchased a radio set and subsequently received a telephone call from the secretary to the German consul, who was interested in the radio. Colepaugh denied building the set but admitted selling it to the German official for sixty dollars. He stated that he had visited the German consulate in Boston on numerous occasions during early 1941.

From January to April 1940, Colepaugh was employed at Lawley's shipyard in the Neponset section of Boston as a laborer on yachts. One of the officials at Lawley's in the year the suspect worked there stated in February 1965 that Colepaugh probably was one of the men who left the yard at once when told they would have to be fingerprinted and photographed. "Several men left in a hurry on learning this information, not even stopping to get their pay," the official explained. Colepaugh is remembered as a thin, mild-mannered youth who would not attract more than average attention.

On May 7, 1941, Colepaugh went to Canada and shipped

out as a seaman on the *Reynolds*. The boat went to Scotland and returned to Boston in the latter part of July 1941. He subsequently landed in New York City and, on September 5, 1941, obtained a job as a deckhand on board the *Anita,* sailing from New York City for Rio de Janeiro. He was at Buenos Aires in October 1941.

On December 8, 1941, the day after the Pearl Harbor attack, Colepaugh secured a position as deckhand on the tanker *William G. Warden*. He made a few trips on this craft in South American waters, and on March 25, 1942, was again in Buenos Aires. On April 5 of the same year, he worked as a deckhand on board the *Scania*.

Colepaugh stated that he had written to the German Library of Information in New York City for publications, and he added that he had attended a birthday celebration in honor of Hitler at the German consulate in Boston. The secretary to the German consulate, according to Colepaugh, had discussed with him the possibility of going to Germany to study at marine engineering schools there.

The United States attorney in Boston advised that he would not authorize prosecution in the case against Colepaugh if he would enlist for military service. Colepaugh promised to do so, and on October 2, 1942, enlisted as an apprentice seaman in the United States Naval Reserve. When he became a member of the armed forces, under the jurisdiction of the Navy, the FBI's case on William Curtis Colepaugh was closed administratively. Copies of Bureau reports were furnished Navy officials.

On June 28, 1943, the FBI received information that Colepaugh had been discharged from the Navy "for the good of the service." Once more he was in civilian life, and again the FBI became interested in his activities.

On March 26, 1943, Colepaugh commenced employment at the Waltham Watch Company in Waltham, Massachusetts. Three months later he was working for a poultry farmer in Concord, Massachusetts.

A check with the local draft board indicated Colepaugh telephoned them on January 10, 1944, that he was going to enter the merchant marine. Five days later the draft board received a letter from him postmarked New York enclosing a note on Swedish American Steamship Line stationery certifying Colepaugh was employed on board the *Gripsholm* as a messboy.

The FBI had been informed that the *Gripsholm* was carrying individuals who were to be repatriated to Germany. It was not known whether Colepaugh would return to the United States as a crew member aboard the same ship. The FBI therefore asked several government agencies to advise the FBI in the event Colepaugh reentered the United States.

On February 15, 1944, the *Gripsholm* sailed. Within a few days of her arrival in Portugal, Colepaugh phoned the German consulate in Lisbon but was advised that the consul was not in. At noon the following day Colepaugh went to the consulate in person. He told the doorman that he was from the *Gripsholm* and wanted to see the consul, explaining that he was a friend of the former German consul in Boston.

Within a relatively short time Colepaugh was interviewed by the German consul and taken to Germany. He was then transported to Security Service headquarters at The Hague in Holland. Here he met Eric Gimpel, who was to become his partner. Gimpel had been an instructor in 1943 at a fascist academy for young boys in Madrid, Spain, after which he returned to Berlin as a prominent member of the Security Service. In Berlin he had been given a private office and a secretary.

Gimpel and Colepaugh began training for the dangerous mission ahead, a mission that would involve crossing the Atlantic in a German submarine and landing on American soil. Courses included radio work and use of firearms and explosives. The American was given a tremendous amount of athletic training to build up his relatively weak body, and he learned to drive a motorcycle. He was taught how to handle explosives and was shown the most effective way to derail a train. He was shown how to handle Thermit, which could burn through metal.

In August Colepaugh and Gimpel went to Berlin for a photographic course, using a Leica camera, that included developing and printing special photographs. Then they went to Dresden, Germany, to study microphotography and learn to work with microphotographic apparatus. They soon were able to reduce regular Leica negatives to sixteen-millimeter film.

In Dresden and later in Berlin, Colepaugh did not know what his assignment would be. Eventually he learned that he was to go to the United States. Two days before Colepaugh and Gimpel left Berlin for Kiel, they were advised that their objective in the United States was to obtain information from periodicals, newspapers, radio and all available sources regarding shipbuilding, airplanes and rockets. Gimpel was to build a special radio that would send information out of the United States. In an emergency they were to use American prisoners of war as "mail drops." Letters sent to these captives were to be written in secret ink. In sending radio information out of the United States, they were to use specific code-wave lengths and times.

Their final instructions included the code for sending radio messages to Germany. It was based on the words, "Lucky Strike cigarettes, it's toasted." They were also furnished wristwatches and two small compasses, as well as two kits of concentrated food taken from captured American pilots.

Gimpel received a blue onionskin paper packet containing about one hundred small diamonds. These were to be used to provide funds in the event the money given to them was found to be worthless or dangerous to use.

Gimpel and Colepaugh signed various identification papers. Those for Colepaugh carried the name William C. Caldwell. The papers consisted of a birth certificate showing Colepaugh to have been born in New Haven, Connecticut; a Selective Service registration card showing him to be registered at Local Board 18, Boston, Massachusetts; a Selective Service classification card from the same draft board; a certificate of discharge from the United States Naval Reserve; and a motor vehicle operator's license for the State of Massachusetts. There were also several duplicate papers, completely signed and filled out except that names and addresses were omitted to permit Colepaugh and Gimpel to assume other names if necessary.

About September 22, 1944, Gimpel and Colepaugh went to Kiel and spent two days waiting aboard the Hamburg-American liner *Milwaukee*. Subsequently they went aboard German submarine *1230,* which left immediately and remained off Kiel for about two days awaiting a German convoy going up the coast of Denmark. They proceeded with this convoy to Horton, Norway, where the submarine was tested for about six days. The next port was Kristiansand, Norway: two days to take on food and fuel.

Colepaugh and Gimpel had received expense money of $60,000, a sum determined when Colepaugh pointed out that the American cost of living had taken a sharp turn upward. He estimated $15,000 a year living expenses for one man in the United States. Based on this, $60,000 was given to them as expenses for two men for a period of two years.

On October 6, 1944, the submarine left Kristiansand bound for the United States. The transatlantic trip was made under conditions of extreme caution.

On November 10, 1944, the Nazi U-boat approached the Grand Banks of Newfoundland. At that point the crew took radio bearings on Boston, Massachusetts, and on Portland and Bangor, Maine. Later they established a position off the Maine coast at Mount Desert Rock. They lay off that point until about 4:00 P.M. on the afternoon of November 29, 1944.

During the day the submarine rested on the ocean bottom. At night it charged its batteries by using Diesel engines. Through listening devices the crew could hear fishing boats on the surface nearby. Throughout one day they had listened to a fishing boat anchored above them. About this time word was received by radio from Berlin that a submarine had been sunk in Frenchman's Bay, Maine. The Captain of the *1230* was instructed to land Colepaugh and Gimpel somewhere other than Frenchman's Bay.

Colepaugh, Gimpel and the captain * of the submarine discussed landing places in Rhode Island, New Hampshire and Maine. Eventually the captain disregarded the instructions from Berlin. On the night of November 29, 1944, the submarine, completely submerged, started for Frenchman's Bay.

About half a mile off Crab Tree Point the captain ordered the craft to be raised until the conning tower was just above water. In this fashion they proceeded to a point about three hundred yards from shore at Crab Tree Point, which is near the peninsula of Hancock Point.

During the trip across the Atlantic, Colepaugh and Gimpel had worn regulation German naval uniforms. About half an hour before the submarine came to its offshore position, they removed the uniforms and donned civilian attire.

The submarine turned to face the south, and the crew made ready a rubber boat with oars. Attached to this boat was a light line to pull the rubber boat back to the submarine after the saboteurs rowed ashore. But when the boat was launched the line broke. It was necessary for two crew members to row the agents to shore and then return in the craft.

At the landing point there was a narrow beach approximately six feet, with a bank above it. In the stillness of that cold November night on the Maine coast, Nazi agents Colepaugh and Gimpel stepped from the rubber boat onto the shores of the United States. The German sailors also went ashore so that they could return to their homeland and brag that they had touched American shores. When these sailors departed they saluted, "Heil Hitler."

With all their equipment, Colepaugh and Gimpel climbed

---

* H. Hilbig, captain of the *U 1230*, surrendered his submarine June 24, 1945, at a time when many others were giving up.

the bank and walked through the woods adjacent to the shoreline until they reached a dirt road. They did not bring any explosives ashore, nor did they bury anything on the beach. In fact, they did not even bring the microphotographic apparatus from the submarine because it was extremely heavy. Gimpel claimed later they were weakened because of their long stay aboard the submarine.

On that night, five months before VE Day, Colepaugh and Gimpel came up a path leading through woods to the road along the west side of Hancock Point. They started on foot down the road toward Hancock shortly before midnight, muffled by a moderate snowfall.

Two Americans soon became aware of their presence. Mrs. Mary Forni, wife of a Franklin, Maine, schoolteacher and the mother of three children, was driving home from a gathering of neighborhood women. She saw two men laden with bundles walking along the high road. Although the men were strangers, she noted nothing suspicious about their actions. A little later Mrs. Forni saw Ellsworth High School senior Harvard M. Hodgkins in his car as he drove home from a dance at Hancock Village. After Mrs. Forni reached home she began to wonder why two strangers should be trudging along late at night in the Hancock Point area at that time of year. If it had been July or August, the height of the summer season, she would not have "given it a second thought."

The more she thought the more it worried her. Finally Mrs. Forni decided to call the Hodgkins's residence the following morning. The lad's father, deputy sheriff Dana Hodgkins, was away on a hunting trip. Mary Forni talked with his wife and asked her to question her son regarding the two men. Harvard Hodgkins confirmed their presence, saying that without question he saw the tracks of the men along the road as he drove home.

That afternoon Deputy Hodgkins returned and immediately began investigating the incident. He followed tracks in the snow down a path at Hancock Point to the water's edge, where he saw enough to convince him that the men had landed from the sea. At first he wondered if the pair could be hunters. But when he saw that the tracks ended at the ocean's edge and noted evidence that a rubber raft had landed, he decided to contact the FBI in Bangor.

Four days after the landing FBI agents questioned Mrs. Forni and the Hodgkins boy. They set in motion machinery that led to the eventual capture of Colepaugh and Gimpel.

The two spies did reach Boston and then New York. But Colepaugh decided to surrender. He aided in capturing Gimpel, after which both were tried and sentenced to be executed as German spies. Their sentences were reduced to imprisonment. They were freed after serving a substantial number of years in prison.

It is believed that later Harvard Hodgkins spent a whirlwind week in New York as guest of a New York newspaper and a radio program of that era. This was at least partly a reward for reporting the spies on November 30, 1944.

I visited Mrs. Forni up on the Hancock Point peninsula. She took me to the very location where the saboteurs from the *U 1230* landed on the beach. Mrs. Forni and Harvard Hodgkins helped make history on that memorable night in 1944 by thwarting one of the most daring spy plots hatched in World War II.

2

Loss
of the *Lakonia*

All seemed in readiness for the cruise ahead. It was December 1963. The location was Southampton, England, where three liners were tied up at Berth 107. Two of the ships were familiar to me—the *Queen Elizabeth* and the *Queen Mary*. The third craft, between the Queens, was the *Lakonia*.

Although the weather was not perfect, it was an average winter day in the British Isles. The 20,314-ton *Lakonia* bore the sea trident as symbol of the liner's company. Ironically, one circular for the cruise ship stressed that the trip was to be a holiday with all risks eliminated.

The 658 passengers were eager to escape England's cold climate in favor of the Canary Islands and Madeira. With the crew of 383, there were 1041 in all, from all walks of life—stewards, chefs, carpenters, hair dressers, electricians, stockbrokers, honeymoon couples, a model, a well-known actor, a schoolmaster, an architect, a baronet, a dentist, army officers, a football club manager, a bookmaker, students, babies, pregnant women, widows and wealthy retired couples. Both the strong and the crippled were aboard.

Most of the passengers knew little of the *Lakonia*'s past history. The Greek liner had been a troubled craft since her launching in 1930. Formerly the Dutch liner *Johan van Oldenbarnevelt,* she had been constructed by the Nederland Shipping Company. On her maiden voyage, with Queen Wilhelmina aboard, she collided with another craft in the North Sea. On one voyage in 1951 six small but dangerous fires broke out. In 1962 she was sold to the Ormos Shipping Company, a Greek firm, which changed her name to *Lakonia* and put her in drydock for refurbishing so that she would be ready for the cruise trade.

The ship and its complement of excited passengers sailed from Southampton with few cares. As a precaution, the captain ordered a fire and boat drill December 22, 1963, while the ship was sailing at a speed of 17 knots. The drill was executed successfully.

At eleven o'clock that evening a steward walking by the barber shop, which was closed, noticed smoke seeping under the door. When he forced entrance to the barber shop, he discovered a wall of flame about to engulf him. Running for help, he found that the fire had already gained terrific headway in the hall, and that the conflagration was heading toward the staterooms.

Meanwhile the skipper, Captain M. N. Zarbis, detected an odor he could not believe—the terrifying, overwhelming smell of smoke. He immediately set about to find the cause of this most feared danger at sea. The alarm was soon sounded, and crew members as well as passengers were seized with some degree of confusion and concern.

A ship's warning system, alerting and in many cases overwhelming each person aboard, is an appalling, startling, frightening noise. In conjunction with the emergency it heralds, the alarm often creates panic. Some on the *Lakonia* did nothing, appearing dazed; others thought of life preservers; still others realized that they were already in immediate danger from the flames. In the dance hall the orchestra tried to keep playing to calm the crowd, but in split seconds the screams and shouts drowned the music.

In the radio room Operator Kalogridis had been flashing out Christmas messages over the airwaves. Suddenly a message from the bridge told him of the blaze. Forgetting the holiday greetings, he ripped out over the air a distress signal, telling all other ships in range that the *Lakonia* desperately needed assistance because the fire was out of control. He gave the ship's position: latitude 35 degrees North, longitude 24 degrees West.

There was panic aboard the *Lakonia*. The lifeboat deck was crowded with crew and passengers scrambling for the rescue craft, stumbling around in every possible attire. Women in evening gowns and men in tuxedos, others in nightgowns and pajamas, forgot everything but the possibility of saving their lives. Great sections of the burning ship were rapidly becoming a blazing inferno. Some lifeboats were launched, but the great swells and December cold jeopardized those lucky enough to be on board. Four of the *Lakonia*'s survival craft could not be dropped to the sea because of the flames and heat. Many discouraged passengers who despaired of getting into lifeboats jumped into the ocean wearing lifejackets. Soon it became a question of how long they—and the lifeboats— could stay afloat.

The first rescue craft was the *Montcalm,* one of the passenger ships called to the scene. Others included the Coast Guard cutter *Mackinac,* the *Salta,* the *Gertrude Frizen,* the *Stratheden,* the British aircraft carrier *Centaur,* the two American liners *Independence* and *Rio Grande,* as well as the Belgian ship *Charlesville.*

As soon as the *Montcalm* reached the scene, searchlights were zigzagged across the water, giving courage and hope to victims in the sea. The rescue ship picked up many people from the water and from the lifeboats. By early dawn the *Montcalm* radioed that 240 had been taken aboard, with 12 dead. Shortly afterward came the *Stratheden*'s report that they had saved 300.

With the coming of morning rescue planes looked down

upon a gruesome sight. One airplane pilot recalled later a dead baby floating all by itself in a lifebelt; the incident simply overwhelmed him.

Except for part of the stern, flames were sweeping the entire *Lakonia*. About a hundred people were crowded around the taffrail, including Captain Zarbis. Then, one by one, they leaped into the sea. Some drowned; others were picked up by one of the eighteen boats helping in the rescue work.

Finally word came that many of those who had been rescued—both members of the ship's company and passengers—were on the way to Casablanca aboard the *Charlesville,* the *Mehdi* or the *Montcalm*. It was Christmas Day when they arrived, and they were given the choice of hotel rooms or air transportation to their homes. Other survivors were taken to Funchal in Madeira. Most were dazed or weeping after suffering hours in lurching lifeboats. Several refused to go on another Greek ship, the *Arkadia,* which was waiting to rush them to Southampton.

The disaster claimed 155 lives; 886 passengers and crewmen survived after very difficult rescue operations. In the tradition of the sea, Captain Zarbis was the last to leave the burning liner.

What caused the fire? There are many different opinions, but overloaded fuses probably were to blame. The countless mistakes by individuals on the ship, timing errors, communication failures and simply bad luck all contributed to the tragedy of the *Lakonia*. The Marine Ministry investigating the fire discovered that when the ship was refurbished, she was not fitted with automatic water sprinklers for use in a fire. This may well have been the deciding reason for her loss.

It was arranged to have the *Lakonia* towed into Gibraltar. But when two tugs, the *Herkules* and the *Polzee,* attempted to tow her, the *Lakonia* went down in two thousand fathoms 250 miles from her destination. This sinking, of course, meant that the exact cause of the blaze would never be known.

Later came the usual charges, complaints, accusations and

denials, as is almost always the case in marine tragedies of this sort. One man said that there were orders and counterorders. Another saw twenty people leaving the ship in a lifeboat built for seventy-five. Still another observer charged that Greek seamen, in panic, fought with passengers for places in the lifeboats.

A passenger stated that members of the crew often did not seem to know what to do in the emergency, and said that they even thought of taking passengers back to the burning vessel. Another testified that almost every member of the crew managed to get aboard the rescue craft before the passengers.

The final decision of the Marine Ministry investigating the actual reactions of the crew who ran the *Lakonia* was that they acted in faultless manner and in accordance with Greek tradition. This is ridiculous.

3

Burning
of a Lighthouse

One of the greatest Englishmen of all times stated more than a quarter century ago that the lifeboat "drives on as a proof, a symbol, a testimony, that man is created in the image of God." Sir Winston Churchill, when he made this statement, said that the lifeboat "drives on with a mercy which does not quail in the presence of death."

Coastguardsmen and lifesavers all deserve great commendation. Two of the most outstanding are Americans Joshua James, who saved 636 lives in his career, and Coxswain Henry Blogg of Cromer, England, who went out on service 387 times and rescued a total of 873 people.

As grateful as anyone for the work of lifesavers were the three keepers of England's Chickens Rock Lighthouse. Off the tip of the Isle of Man lies an island called the Calf of Man. To the southwest is a reef where the Chickens Rock Lighthouse was built more than a century ago. Extending 149 feet into the air, the tower was surrounded by water at high tide.

On December 23, 1960, the British Admiralty sent out a warning to all vessels that disaster had struck that lighthouse, extinguishing the light. Exact details of what caused the fire were never made clear. But it is known that at approximately ten-thirty in the morning a terrific explosion occurred at the Chickens Rock Light, setting the inside of the tower ablaze within minutes. At the time of the explosion all three keepers were high in the tower in one of the upper rooms. They were trapped by the flames below. It looked as if they would be burned alive.

Means of escape were present, however. The three keepers tied a rope to the ironwork of the upper balcony where they were imprisoned, then used the long line to reach relative safety at the base of the tower. One of the men sustained ugly burns sliding down the line.

Although they had reached temporary safety, matters grew dangerously critical as time went by. The force of the wind was increasing, which would make rescue impossible. And the men realized that the coming high tide would inundate them.

Minute by minute the wind was growing stronger. Above them the flames sweeping the lighthouse were approaching the storage tanks, which meant that another blinding explosion was imminent. Half-dressed, the keepers were suffering from the bitter cold and swirling surf.

Then the three keepers saw a boat approaching, tossing in the gathering wind. The craft was the Royal Navy National Lifeboat Institution's *R. A. Colby Cubbin.*

The *Cubbin* had steamed away from Port St. Mary at 11:10 that morning after hearing of the trouble. At first the authorities did not know quite what had happened and what could be done. Then came word that the three keepers were safe temporarily at the burning lighthouse but had to be rescued almost at once because of the rising tide. The *Cubbin* lost no time in getting to the tower.

Watching carefully as the red, white and blue lifeboat with the servicemen dressed in their yellow oilskins approached the lighthouse, the keepers wondered how they could possibly save their lives before the rising wind, waves and tide made it too late.

By now the three men had been forced to climb back onto the lower part of the tower. They clung to a small emergency landing stage, the water just a few inches below, spraying them with every wave. Since the boiling surf as well as the hidden boulders prevented the *Cubbin* from getting closer than three hundred feet, Coxswain Gawne readied his gun to fire the line in such a way that the three keepers could be saved.

Then the loudspeaker from the *Cubbin* advised the men imprisoned at the base of the burning lighthouse to secure one end of a sturdy line to the tower and attach the other end to a board they would throw into the sea. When this was done the board rapidly floated away from the tower. Another line fired from the lifeboat landed in the water across the one the keepers had sent out. Within a short time the men in the lifeboat had pulled the rope in so that they were connected to the tower.

The keepers now hauled back the original line, bringing back the lifeboat line and the breeches buoy as well. The end of the breeches buoy rope was then strapped to the iron lighthouse ladder.

The men had agreed that the keeper who had burned his hands should be given the first trip across to safety. Within ten minutes the two other lighthouse men had strapped him safely to the buoy and started him off for the lifeboat. Unfortunately, when he was halfway across to the *Cubbin,* a giant wave smashed against the breeches buoy, capsizing it and throwing the keeper into the water. With great difficulty the men from the *Cubbin* managed to reach him. Pulling the keeper aboard, they wrapped him in a blanket and took him below, where they kept him warm near the engines. He suffered severely from his burns, exposure and general shock.

There was still the problem of rescuing the two remaining lighthouse keepers. The captain of the *Cubbin* decided to send for help. Not trusting the breeches buoy after the capsizing, he radioed for assistance from the Port Erin lifeboat *Matthew*

Simpson. She was launched at once. Meanwhile the *Cubbin* made for Port Erin as quickly as possible to land the rescued keeper, who required immediate medical attention.

The *Matthew Simpson* soon reached the scene of the smoking tower. They found the situation even worse than before but could only stand by in case the two keepers should need emergency assistance before the *Cubbin* returned.

It was now decided to dispatch an Air Force rescue helicopter from Anglesey. The craft was soon hovering near the burning tower. The pilot realized that the only safe way he could remove the men was to lift them off the upper lighthouse balcony. But he also knew there was no way the keepers could climb again through the flames to the top of the structure. With deep regret he returned to his station.

Thus the only solution was for the lifeboats to find some way to take the men off Chickens Rock.

By this time a sizable gathering had assembled on a hill on the Isle of Man. They stood staring out at the tall tower with smoke billowing through the windows. At the base every wave brought white seething foam, which now covered the lower part of the light where the men clung desperately to the ladder. By this time the two lifeboats had arrived back at the reef. The lifesavers could do nothing as the waves roared in around the structure, swirling over the dangerous rocks. The two craft, the *Cubbin* and the *Matthew Simpson,* maneuvered helplessly off the light for the next three hours, unable to approach closer than a hundred yards.

Then came the change of tide, and the lower area around the base of the lighthouse began to reveal itself. The weather also had moderated. With the Port Erin lifeboat, *Matthew Simpson,* standing by, the *Cubbin* cautiously approached the base of the tower, came alongside and managed to rescue the two keepers. The men had been on the burning tower and reef for more than eight hours, half-dressed, with wind and spray numbing them. Now, wrapped in heavy blankets, they were placed below near the engine's warmth.

Still burning away, the lighthouse faded into the distance as the rescuers returned to shore with the keepers. All night the Chickens Rock Lighthouse sent up wisps of smoke from the blackened windows, the tower standing lonely and forgotten on the location it had protected for more than eighty-five years.

Two days went by, and then the lighthouse tender *Hesperus* * arrived off the burned tower, sailing to the area from Oban. She placed a flashing beacon in the vicinity of the fire-blackened tower to warn all shipping away from the reef. The tower itself stood as a reminder of the explosion and of the catastrophe averted by so narrow a margin. The incident proved once more the statements of Sir Winston Churchill.

* Whether or not the *Hesperus* was the same tender that participated in the strangest incident ever in the history of the service is unclear. On December 26, 1900, the tender *Hesperus* stopped at Eileen Noors Lighthouse in the Hebrides and discovered that the three keepers were missing. Although search was made for months, they were never found.

4

Trapped Aboard
the *Kaptajn Nielsen*

The rescue of people trapped under the ocean's surface is always noteworthy and fascinating. The miraculous escape from the *Adelaide*, capsized near Barnegat Light, is told in Part III of this book. Here is the tale of the giant dredge *Kaptajn Nielsen*, which sank to the bottom of Australia's Brisbane Harbor in September 1964. Thirty-three men were imprisoned at the bottom of the sea under circumstances rarely equaled in the world's marine history. Eight of the victims died almost at once. Efforts were made to rescue the others, who were kept alive by air trapped inside the craft.

The disaster that befell the Danish dredge occurred late in the evening of Friday, September 18, 1964. First sign on shore that something was amiss was at 11:30, when vacationer Bob Anthony was gazing out from the Tangalooma tourist resort. He saw "what looked like searchlights" and a long cigar-shaped vessel in the channel between Moreton Island and the mainland. He dismissed it as a "submarine" and went to bed.

It was not until 3:00 A.M. Saturday morning that Seaman Eric Poulsen, after an incredible four-mile swim followed by a two-mile staggering run on the beach, reached Moreton Island in Brisbane Harbor to report the tragedy and ask for help.

Dressed in only his soaking wet underpants and a polo shirt, his feet cut and bleeding, Poulsen stumbled to the first cottage he saw and knocked on the door. "Boat overturn . . . many drown . . . telephone," he said in broken English to the occupant, Mrs. Bennett, when she answered his knock.

"I thought he was a drunk," Mrs. Bennett later recalled. "I was a bit scared, so I closed the door and went to tell my husband. But Poulsen kept knocking, and when we had a good look at him we realized something terrible had happened."

Mr. William Isherwood, at the Tangalooma tourist resort, reported to the Water Police that a man named Eric Poulsen was reporting that the great dredge in the harbor had turned turtle.

"We thought it was a joke," said Sergeant Jim Schofield of the Water Police. "But I checked it out and found the dredge was overdue. We immediately organized rescue operations." Word had reached him at 3:05 A.M. Saturday.

In a short time the air was filled with police appeals broadcast on every radio station in the vicinity. Owners of outboard motorboats, cabin cruisers and work boats were beseeched to go out to the disaster scene. Sergeant Les Clark of the Water Police notified all civilian skin divers that they were desperately needed.

The response was amazing and gratifying, the start of a massive rescue operation. Dozens of craft, including launches, speedboats, trawlers and tugs, soon converged on the area. The most vital move was made by a scuba diving organization headed by Joe Engwirda, thirty-two, a professional who ran a school for underwater divers in Brisbane. Arriving on the scene with great haste, he actively supervised the rescue. It was a situation no scuba diver had ever faced before.

In nighttime's pitch darkness, under the surface of the ocean, the divers explored the overturned craft foot by foot. With the help of electric torches, they discovered that the steel plates had burst in two when the giant dredge capsized, and several doors had broken from their hinges. Fighting their way through the overturned craft, Engwirda and the other scuba divers reached the survivors in cabins that were half-filled with water. There was still enough trapped air to keep the sailors alive.

"They were panicky when I first got there," explained Engwirda. "I had to spend about a half hour talking to the sailors before I brought them out. Fortunately I speak a bit of Danish.

"We got Aqualungs for the trapped men to come up with. I gave the crewmen a quick lesson on using the Aqualungs and let each one have a short workout in the cabin before we tried to get out.

"We had to take the men out through a skylight only three feet wide. In the middle of the skylight was a steel bar that we could not get through with our Aqualung equipment on. We had to take off our Aqualungs to pass through and then put them back on again. We had trouble pulling the men through the skylight. One chap was too fat to get through and he panicked, but he finally escaped. On the average it only took two minutes to get each man from his cabin to the surface. We used air hoses for panicky ones who could not be given Aqualungs." Air was also sent into the hull to replenish the supply.

Senior Constable Ivan Adams also covered himself with glory that September morning, bringing up several survivors. He said, "Trouble was that most of the trapped men had not used underwater gear before. One of the men refused to use gear at all. I grabbed hold of him, told him to take a breath, and got him out as quickly as possible. The door of the cabin had been smashed, and we had to tear it away to get into that particular cabin. We had to rip furniture from around another man who was trapped in his cabin."

After being underwater for more than four hours, the constable collapsed. It was found that he had developed a severe carbon dioxide headache from the impure air in the ship. He and Engwirda had been the first skin divers on the scene. Adams said later that the superstructure and bridge of the dredge were buried in the sand, and the ship was fast on the bottom.

At 2:00 P.M. the afternoon following the disaster, Water Police Sergeant Schofield, in overall charge of rescue work, gave up all hope of finding more survivors and announced discontinuance of operations. Sergeant Schofield said: "There is definitely no one left alive on board. A dozen skin divers have just searched the length and breadth of the ship. They went into every nook and cranny, every cabin, every alleyway, dining room and engine room. They tapped in each section of the ship but got no response. Then they repeated the search, just to make sure. They are satisfied there is no person alive aboard the ship."

Sergeant Schofield emphasized the fact that fifteen crewmen escaped. It was "the greatest stroke of good luck I have seen in many a day," he said. When the tragedy occurred, he reported, the dredge was taking on sand and had almost completed a capacity loading. Schofield added that it was his opinion the dredge turned over suddenly. "It just went 'whoof.' "

The survivors later related what their thoughts and actions had been while they were imprisoned in the dredge. Electrical engineer Kim Petersen, thirty-six, the last to leave the underwater tomb, told his rescuers the following day that there was no panic. This seems to contradict what diver Joe Engwirda reported; possibly conditions varied in different parts of the submerged craft.

"Even when things looked the worst," said Petersen, "we were confident you would get us out somehow. I promised the boys that we could stay alive at least two days. Maybe I was a bit optimistic."

Petersen praised the spirit of all the survivors, particularly several young crew members. Even when the water was rising and the air getting stale, they kept their heads and managed to tell a joke or two.

"I was sitting on my bunk," said Petersen, "when the dredge lurched over. I managed to drag myself through the cabin door. Just as the lights failed I saw James Madsen, a young Danish apprentice, madly scrambling up the living quarter steps.

"Madsen was met by a wall of water and disappeared. He drowned. I and eight others managed to climb into an up-turned cabin that contained a trapped air bubble. When the water settled, clusters of phosphorescent organisms gave us a little light to see with.

"I tapped a chair leg on a table for three hours to let anyone outside the hull know that we were still alive. After three hours my prayers were answered when a tap-tap-tap rang through from outside the keel. Incidentally, several of the men had been bruised when the barge capsized, and were bleeding; some were worried that the blood might attract sharks.

"All the time we were peering into the water waiting for divers to reach us. It was a terrific feeling when the first frog-man came through a skylight under us in the cabin roof."

The first survivor to be rescued was Per Wistensen, a fifteen-year-old cabin boy. Then came oiler Gurg Jakobsen, fifty-eight, the oldest man in the cabin. Others followed. Petersen was the last to be rescued, for he had volunteered to show young crew members how to use the air equipment.

For the *Kaptajn Nielsen*'s chief cook, fifty-two-year-old Aage Hansen of Rudkjobling, it was the third time he had been lucky. Hansen, one of the men entombed for eight hours in the flooded cabin, had a previous record of shipwrecks at sea.

Waiting to have a gash on his forehead treated at the General Hospital, Hansen showed a large scar on his right arm. "Mussolini gave this to me when one of his planes bombed our ship out of the water during the Spanish civil war. Then in 1942, during Hitler's war, my boat went down off Greenland after it struck a rock, and we were stranded in Greenland for three months. But last night was easily the worst experience I had at sea.

"In my bunk when the dredge turned over, I was stunned by a blow on the head. One of the cabin doors flew off its hinges, and I found myself floating down a passageway. I swam and paddled into another cabin where there was not so much water, and there were my mates.

"The spirit of the boys was wonderful, especially that of the young ones. During the night they sang songs and some even told jokes." Hansen said he would be going back to sea as soon as he returned to Denmark. "It's my living," he asserted.

Deckhand Dion Jorgensen, seventeen, from Aarlborg, Denmark, said he heard three men drown shortly after the dredge capsized. "They were calling for help, but we couldn't do anything." Jorgensen said nine seamen crammed into his cabin as a wall of water bore down on them when the dredge went over. "We thought we were going to die. Nine of us stood in water about four and a half feet deep. We were in that room for eight hours."

Rescue from the deathtrap hull came as a birthday present for Gurg Jakobsen, an oiler from Copenhagen. "Today is my fifty-eighth birthday," Jakobsen said at the General Hospital.

Engineroom-hand Christian Reinholdt arrived at the Brisbane General Hospital semiconscious from immersion and shock. Others taken to the hospital were the captain of the dredge, Karl Albert Flindt, and the second officer, Niels Sonne. Reinholdt and Sonne were picked up by a helicopter piloted by Captain Ray Hudson. The chopper landed on the water near the disaster scene, then sped the survivors to a hospital.

Two survivors, Svend Frederiksen, twenty-six, and Borje Hanson, forty-four, missed certain death by a bare six inches. They climbed out through a pipe and were sitting on the overturned hull when help arrived.

"In seconds," Frederiksen explained later, "the water rushed in and then all the lights went out. I found myself down in the main engine room, swimming in the darkness. The water was covered with oil from the Diesel and lubricating tanks. I swam over to Hanson, and we climbed up on one of the engines to try to get out of the water. It was dark and cold, and the water was rising all the time.

"I found one of the engine room tools and banged on the hull, but there was no answer. The stern end was getting deeper, so we swam forward. We heard hissing as air trapped in the compartment began escaping. It came from one of the big tubes through which sand is pumped when dredging. We decided to get into the tube. If we opened it and it was full of water, we would drown for sure.

"Our air was nearly gone and the water was up to our chests, so we risked it and tore it open. We could see the end of the tube about eighteen feet ahead. Most of it was underwater, but the top of the tube was six inches clear. We crawled along it, keeping our heads out of the water, then ducked down and swam out. We sat on the keel waving the flashlight but could not attract anyone's attention, though we could see people on shore. Finally we were rescued."

A three-day hearing was held later in the year before shipping inspector Captain R. Hildebrand and a battery of legal and shipping representatives. First there was an announcement that the body of one of the two men still missing had been found by a private launch in Moreton Bay. It was identified as James Madsen.

Master of the *Kaptajn Nielsen*, Captain Karl Albert Flindt, forty-three, was the first witness heard. "About 11:15 P.M. I left the bridge to go to my day room," he said. "I heard the sound of the winches commencing to raise the suction pipe on the starboard side. The ship started to hang over slightly. This is usual when the suction pipe is being raised. Normally the ship settles back again. This time she didn't.

"She did not stop going to starboard. At first she moved only slightly, then faster. I became alarmed. I decided to go back to the bridge to see what was happening."

Captain Flindt said that he reached the door of his day room and was "thrown back inside by a wall of water."

The officer of the watch, First Mate M. Munt, and the winchman, Mr. Eschen, both of whom were on the bridge, were killed. Mr. Eschen, who had been operating the dredging controls, had twenty years experience.

Captain Flindt said he did not believe the dredge was overloaded. He had looked at the load meter before leaving the bridge, and it indicated that the loading was nearly completed. Captain Hildebrand asked Captain Flindt if he had ever known a loading meter to "go wrong." Flindt said it had happened once on the *Kaptajn Nielsen,* but a long time ago. "I don't think it went wrong on this occasion," he added. Captain Flindt said he had no idea why the dredge capsized.

Professional skin diver Joe Engwirda, in testifying before Captain Hildebrand, said that he believed the capsizing of the *Kaptajn Nielsen* took no more than ten seconds. He based his opinion on observations he made while diving into the semisubmerged dredge. Engwirda found that furniture drawers which could have moved to starboard had not had time to slide out of position. He tested the drawers and they moved easily. He added: "Another reason for my opinion is that the ship filled with water so quickly that a lot of the crockery was still unbroken." The water came in so fast that when the crockery shifted at the moment the dredge capsized, the dishes fell into water instead of onto the metal deck.

Engwirda said he also considered that from the time the dredge began to capsize to the moment it completely turned over, it had not moved more than ten feet from the location over which it was working. He deduced this from the debris beneath the ship on the sea bottom.

Engwirda said that the engine room telegraph on the bridge was at "slow ahead" for one engine and at "half ahead" for the other. He had seen this when he first dived into the bridge house. "They have since been moved," he said, "I don't know by whom, but someone must have been playing around with them." He also added that the covering glass on the load meter was broken "by someone or something" after it was taken from the dredge and placed in a small surface boat.

At the time of the capsizing Constable Ivan J. Adams of the Water Police contacted Engwirda, and they used the diver's speedboat to reach the scene at about 7:00 A.M. He said the ship was "anchored" in the sand, principally by the bridge, the funnel, and the masts and gantries. "I did not observe any marks on the hull which might indicate that the ship might have grounded," he added. "Neither did I see any cracked plates or dents on the hull. I also examined the chains support-ing the hopper doors. All locking pins were in place, while the ship's suction pipe was still attached. The head of the pipe was also connected and in one piece."

Constable Adams explained that the lifting wires were lying in the sand, but he could see no breaks. He added that "on the bridge I saw a series of levers with black knobs. All were in a neutral position except one. This was pulled back and I could read the inscription that said: 'Use only with key.' There were a considerable number of spare pieces of gear, steel plate, chains, nuts and bolts lying on the seabed. I could not see the anchors or cables on the bottom, but the lifeboats were still attached to their davits."

The capsizing of the dredge *Kaptajn Nielsen* has never been fully explained. The fact that the vessel's main hopper door chains were still intact exploded the theory that the disaster was caused when those doors suddenly opened, dumping half the dredge's load. Nevertheless, the majority of mariners who studied testimony at the various post-accident hearings agree there was much that could never be either proved or under-stood concerning this strange marine disaster.

Long after other incidents in connection with this tragedy are forgotten, the astounding feat of Seaman Eric Poulsen that terrifying night will be recalled. His remarkable swim and run along the beach to obtain aid rank high in heroism and brav-ery.

Index